D1569144

Global News

Unless Recalled Earlier

DATE DUE

AUG − 9 2002	

Global

News

Perspectives on
the Information Age

Edited by

TONY
SILVIA

Iowa State University Press / Ames

Tony Silvia, Ph.D., is chair of the Journalism Department and a professor of journalism and communication studies at the University of Rhode Island. He teaches television news, broadcasting history, media ethics and literary journalism. He also is a recipient of the 1996 CNN Faculty Fellowship, an honor that led to his reporting as a CNN correspondent that year. His CNN work led to a national award the following year from the Broadcast Education Association. He has worked in local television news as a political, legal and consumer reporter. He is coauthor of *Student Television in America: Channels of Change* (Iowa State University Press, 1998).

© 2001 Iowa State University Press
All rights reserved

Iowa State University Press
2121 South State Avenue, Ames, Iowa 50014

Orders: 1-800-862-6657
Office: 1-515-292-0140
Fax: 1-515-292-3348
Web site: www.isupress.com

Authorization to photocopy items for internal or personal use, or the internal or personal use of specific clients, is granted by Iowa State University Press, provided that the base fee of $.10 per copy is paid directly to the Copyright Clearance Center, 222 Rosewood Drive, Danvers, MA 01923. For those organizations that have been granted a photocopy license by CCC, a separate system of payments has been arranged. The fee code for users of the Transactional Reporting Service is 0-8138-0256-3/2001 $.10.

♾ Printed on acid-free paper in the United States of America

First edition, 1971
Second edition, 2001

Library of Congress Cataloging-in-Publication Data

Global news : perspectives on the information age / edited by Tony Silvia.—2nd ed.
     p. cm.
     Includes bibliographical references and index.
     ISBN 0-8138-0256-3
     1. Television broadcasting of news. 2. Radio journalism. 3. Electronic journals. 4. Journalism. I. Silvia, Tony.

PN 4784.T4 G54 2001
070.1′95—dc21   00-054152

The last digit is the print number: 9 8 7 6 5 4 3 2 1

CONTENTS

Contents

Foreword: The World Today

by Wolf Blitzer

A continuing assault on my profession is underway. Journalists have been targeted around the world. It's dangerous to be a reporter on the front lines of ethnic and political conflict–whether in Africa, the Balkans, Chechnya, the Far East or the Middle East.

U.N. Secretary General Kofi Annan recently summed the impact of this violence up this way: "Each time a journalist is killed or attacked, society at large suffers a grievous wound." The same is true when a struggling newspaper is shut down anywhere in the world because the political powers that be don't like what it's reporting, or when an aggressive television or radio station is silenced because someone in power gets irritated.

And in this new age of the Internet, we must make sure that angry and misguided hackers don't disrupt the power of free speech and free access to information. I see no difference between those who would try to stop a newspaper from running its printing presses or use electronic scrambling devices to prevent a television station from airing the news and those who would try to disrupt the Internet, including governments fearful of allowing their people access to independent information.

Wolf Blitzer is an anchor for CNN's "The World Today," CNN's flagship newscast, as well as the host of "Late Edition with Wolf Blitzer," the only Sunday talk show seen in more than 210 countries. Most recently, he served as CNN's senior White House correspondent. For more than two decades, he has reported on a wide range of major breaking stories around the world, joining CNN in 1990 as the network's military affairs correspondent at the Pentagon.

He is the author of two books, *Between Washington and Jerusalem: A Reporter's Notebook* (Oxford University Press, 1985) and *Territory of Lies* (Harper and Row, 1989), cited by The New York Times Book Review as one of the most notable books of 1989. He also has written articles for numerous publications, including the *New York Times, Washington Post, Wall Street Journal* and *Los Angeles Times.*

We must always be on our guard to ensure that free speech and a free press grow rather than shrink. When it comes to global news, the news is both good and bad. As someone involved in broadcast journalism, I am reminded of the profound words of the singer Marilyn Manson in 1999: "Times have not become more violent. They have just become more televised." As one who works in television, I am very aware that this is so true.

Today, we see shootings, killings and warfare on television—often live. But let's not kid ourselves; people have always been doing these kinds of horrendous things. On my TV program, I have often heard public officials state that we ended the 20th century just as we began it. I would argue that we might have ended it measurably worse.

At the end of the 19th century, Europe had not known a continental war for 85 years. People had a certain self-deception about war and fighting, an infatuation with conflict, which explains in part why they were so thrilled when the soldiers marched off to war in 1914.

But after the bloodiest century in history, we do not have the excuse of ignorance that our predecessors might have offered a hundred years ago. At that time, the world did not know about death camps, about strafing, about poison gas, and certainly not about nuclear war. They had not experienced Leninism or Stalinism or Nazism or the totalitarian state. They could still describe the contest of nations as "The Great Game." We know now it was no game at all. In this age of instant global news, there are no excuses for claiming "We just didn't know."

We know what's going on around the world today. Unfortunately, we don't pay enough attention to global flash points.

• One million North Korean troops still sit along the Demilitarized Zone on the Korean peninsula, only miles away from 40,000 American soldiers and even closer to their own starving countrymen.

• Russia is still unstable, having exploding corruption, thousands of nuclear missiles and an even greater number of scientists and military officers who aren't getting paid.

• More than a billion Chinese are told nothing about ethnic cleansing in Kosovo and everything about a supposed U.S. plot to target their embassy in Belgrade.

• Iraq continues its pursuit of long-range missiles and weapons of mass destruction, including chemical, biological and nuclear, in the absence of U.N. weapons inspection teams.

• And international terrorist organizations, some with state sponsorship, violently focus the alienation of ordinary people toward the supposed cause of their troubles, which is almost always the United States, Israel, and Western culture.

As someone who works for CNN, I am very familiar with these facts and the coverage we give them. Sometimes our reports resonate for the better, when elections in one country can inspire a dozen elections elsewhere. But they often do not, when ethnic cleansing, unchecked and unchallenged, emboldens a dictator to expel a people or worse.

I was in Moscow in March of 2000 covering the Russian elections and arguably the number one threat to our national security today: the so-called loose nukes situation there. Russia still has thousands of nuclear warheads and more than a thousand tons of highly enriched uranium and plutonium, though no one seems to have an exact accounting.

Since 1991, the United States has approved nearly five billion dollars to help secure the nuclear situation in Russia and the other republics of the former Soviet Union. But enormous problems remain and much more money is needed. Don't count on Russia to come up with it.

The enormity of the problem was underlined with the tragedy of the sunken Russian submarine, Kursk. Russian officials had told me previously that their biggest military challenge involves the more than 150 old nuclear-powered submarines that are docked and no longer in service. U.S. funding helped finance the dismantling of a dozen submarines so far, but it will cost billions more to complete the project. The Russians say they have no money to dismantle the submarines and safely store their nuclear reactors and fuel rods. If nothing is done, the subs and their radioactive equipment could eventually sink. At risk: the environment of the ocean bottom reaching all around the world.

The world today–even after the cold war–remains a very dangerous place. The burden is on us as journalists to report on what's going on. The Holocaust was the worst crime against humanity. Since then, people all over the world vowed Never Again. But since World War II, other crimes against humanity have not been lacking, whether it happened:

• 30 years ago in Africa, where more than a million Biafrans were slaughtered;
• or 20 years ago in Cambodia, where the Khmer Rouge slaughtered two million people;
• or more recently–indeed only five years ago–in Rwanda and Burundi, where half a million people were killed in only a few months.

In 1998, I traveled to Africa with President Clinton and met with survivors–members of the Tutsi minority who had been attacked by the Hutu majority. The Hutus killed more people on an hourly and daily basis–often with primitive means such as swords and machetes–than during the Nazis' highly tuned death camps during the Holocaust. This was only five years ago.

Yes, the world is dangerous and yes all the proper lessons still have not been learned. But progress does happen. Right does triumph, sometimes with the help of aggressive global newsgathering.

Through aggressive reporting, we distance ourselves in the most fundamental way from the people who witnessed massacres and did nothing; who heard stories of concentration camps and gas chambers but ignored them; who carried torches and banners mindlessly; who heard the harangues and went along–and in so doing let history happen to them and to others.

As someone who has worked in journalism for nearly 30 years, from locations such as the White House to the Pentagon to the Middle East and beyond and in various media from print to radio to television and now to the Internet, reading *Global News: Perspectives on the Information Age* has been a wonderful and challenging experience. I learned something in almost every chapter, including the observations of Tom Johnson, not only because he's my boss at CNN but also because he's one of the best journalists of our age. Tony Silvia, a highly respected journalism educator, saw firsthand what we do at CNN; he is to be commended for putting all of this together in such a useable form.

Global News: Perspectives on the Information Age will help both veteran and new reporters better understand the rapidly changing world in which we live. It is well-written, solidly edited, and very useful for both the professional journalist as well as those who are simply interested in the evolving impact of the news media. I have seen enormous technological changes during my career in journalism, but my sense is the biggest changes are just around the corner. Only a few years from now, we will probably recognize that at the turn of the century–right now–we were at a very primitive stage in the development of the Internet. So read this book–and learn.

Preface

The year was 1996. An early morning phone call resulted in my son, Corey, yelling to me as I struggled to awaken in the midst of my morning shower. "Dad," he said, "it's some guy from Atlanta." I remember saying something like "Atlanta? I don't know anyone in Atlanta. Ask who it is." A moment later, Corey returned with the answer: "He says he's from CNN." It was enough to get me out of the shower and on the phone. I vaguely remembered applying for some form of fellowship with CNN, but it had been six months or more earlier. If I'd thought about it at all during the intervening time, I must have assumed I wasn't selected.

On the other end of the phone was Charlie Caudill, then a senior producer at CNN. I remember his words vividly: "How'd you like to come down here and work with us in Atlanta?" Suddenly, I recalled the terms of what was called the CNN Faculty Fellowship: the opportunity to leave one's position at the university, move to Atlanta, and work as a member of the CNN news gathering and reporting team. After receiving a sabbatical from the University of Rhode Island, I would move to Atlanta that fall and spend a half of a year learning how the CNN networks operate, from both a journalistic and a business perspective. The idea was that I would bring that experience back to my students in the classroom.

The one thing I couldn't have envisioned on the day of that phone call is how the experience would change my life, as both a journalist and a journalism educator. It was pivotal on so many levels and continues to define many aspects of my teaching and writing careers. It was during this time in 1996, when I had the opportunity and the privilege to work with the many stellar journalists at CNN, that the idea for this book was conceived. The newsroom conversations in which I took part convinced me that there was a need for a book–a more permanent connection between working journalists and academic scholars. That book would focus on the exchange of perspectives regarding how, and sometimes why, we report the news for an audience spanning the globe.

While working both as a writer in the CNN newsroom and as a correspondent in its features unit, I would often be in awe of a news agency with such power and reach. The very idea that my stories would be seen and heard by millions of people in countries I would never visit (and some of which I had never even heard) also brought with it a strong sense of responsibility. That shared sense of responsibility among those with whom I worked daily at CNN greatly influenced this book's development.

A series of lectures titled "Global News: the Business of Informing the World" that took place at the University of Rhode Island in the spring of 1998 was another interim step in the book's development. Several of my CNN colleagues took part, as did writers, producers, editors and reporters from MSNBC, the Associated Press and National Public Radio. I am pleased that some of the presenters from that forum have consented to have their work appear in this volume.

Finally, two things seem significant to me about how this book was written. First, few of the authors know each other, fewer still have ever met, and I have actually met only about two-thirds of the contributors. Still, as you read their views on the global news process, I believe you'll be struck, as I was, by how often they agree on fundamental issues. While their contributions were written separately, thousands of miles apart, I believe they tell a combined story of dedication to the principles that guide what some call the craft, others the profession, of reporting. A sincere desire to do better unites these authors, the kind of desire for self-improvement that sometimes elevates journalism to the level of a mission for those who practice it with the greatest skill.

Second, this book never could have been written, certainly not in the form in which it now exists, without the advent of the Internet. Most of the chapters were written, edited, rewritten, and transmitted electronically. That fact alone speaks volumes about the

Internet's potential for sharing information and knowledge toward the improvement of, among other aspects of our world, the practice of journalism.

To some extent, the actualization of this goal may be generational. Our 15-year-old son is already a columnist for an Internet Web site and communicates via e-mail with literally hundreds of readers from around the world everyday. Casey, our college-age daughter, uses the Internet to disperse knowledge about political candidates across the globe via a Web site operated by a group called "Project Vote Smart." Neither aspires to be a journalist in the traditional sense, but both, like many of their generation, know the Internet's important role as a medium for global understanding. In many ways, a similar vision inspired a young Ted Turner to envision and develop CNN. I hope that this book contributes in some meaningful way to that vision.

Acknowledgments

I am indebted to many dedicated journalists at the CNN networks in Atlanta whose work excited, energized, and inspired me during my stay there as a CNN Faculty Fellow in 1996, including former CNN producer Charlie Caudill, who selected me. In particular, I owe a debt of gratitude to CNN President and CEO Tom Johnson, who made me feel welcome as a part of the "Turner Family" and gave me the means and the encouragement to explore any and all areas of the network's operations. He only asked that I leave CNN a better place when I left it; I hope this book is part of fulfilling that promise, Tom.

Others in Atlanta I must thank include Bob Furnad, now president of Headline News, for generously giving his time and sharing his insight into the news business—and for allowing me to report on-air at CNN. I also owe a great deal to my dear friend Ann Kellan, CNN science-technology correspondent, for her encouragement and guidance while I worked as a correspondent in her unit, as well as to former CNN producer Bailey Barash, who helped make my work better by offering an expert eye and a willing ear. Libby Davis, of Turner Learning Services, helped me adapt to life in a new city, even finding me an apartment long before I arrived. I will always be grateful.

CNN writer Glenn Emery showed me the "ropes" early in the process, as did Clint Deloatch and so many others whose patience with me can never be reciprocated. Lou Waters, Natalie Allen, Donna Kelly, Bobbie Batista, Miles O'Brien, Joie Chen, and Bernard Shaw, among the other on-air CNN personnel, all welcomed me and made me feel like an important part of the process—even if Mr. Shaw insisted on referring to me regularly as "the professor!" To Rick Davis of CNN Corporate Communications, thanks are due for believing in this book's worth and for helping recruit Wolf Blitzer to write the foreword.

Outside of CNN, my thanks to Kristine Hendrickson of Salve
Regina University, a wonderful friend and colleague whose support
for this project began with her attending nearly all of the lectures
that were its foundation, in addition to suggesting and securing several of the speakers. Thanks are due to Mel Felner of URI for rescu-
ing me from several computer glitches that threatened to sink the
final draft, and to Ellyn Cardillo, our department secretary, for going
above and beyond to help with the small details that a book requires
in its final prepublication days. The support and understanding of
Judi Brown of ISU Press, an old friend, and Anne Bolen, a new one,
have been indispensable. Finally, to Regina, Casey, and Corey–above
all, this one's for you.

Introduction: Toward a Definition of Global News

Tony Silvia

I remember one of my first news directors in television reciting the well-worn litany of broadcast journalism to me: "News is what people care about and that's basically three things: the fire down the street, the latest movie that everyone wants to see this weekend, and the best beer or soft drink to buy." As a young reporter, I didn't fully comprehend the representative nature of each of those categories. What he was trying to tell me was that I couldn't go wrong by staying focused on (1) what was within a viewer's direct frame of reference or experience (the fire he or she passed on the way home or could see from his window), (2) a more or less guaranteed shared cultural experience (the movie everyone was standing in line and holding up traffic to get in to see) or (3) what are commonly referred to as "pocket book" issues: those stories that direct us to the most value for our hard-earned dollars (the best beer or soft drink to buy).

Today, this definition of what concerns an audience seems at best provincial, at worst woefully incomplete. Still, by comparison,

Dr. Tony Silvia is a professor of Journalism and Communication Studies and chair of the Department of Journalism at the University of Rhode Island. Professor Silvia has taught in the university's journalism department since 1988, primarily in the areas of broadcast journalism, media ethics, broadcasting history and literary journalism. He is the author of more than two dozen nationally published articles in his field, and the author of two books, *Student Television in America: Channels of Change* (1998) and *Global News: Perspectives on the Information Age* (2000). Professor Silvia received a Broadcast Education Association Award for work done as a CNN correspondent while on sabbatical in 1996, the same year he was the recipient of a CNN Faculty Fellowship. He serves on the advisory board of CNN-SB, the Turner Network's student-run news bureau network, as well as on the editorial board of several national academic journals.

it is not nearly as elitist as a definition of news received from a different news director years later. In response to my fear that many of the stories I was reporting didn't really constitute meaningful, important news coverage, that particular news executive looked me straight in the eye and replied: "News is what we say it is; they don't know what's news until we tell them." I was incredulous. By this time in my reporting career, I had covered enough stories to flinch at what I perceived to be the extreme arrogance of such a statement. The reality was that, for its time, the statement was totally true.

It was the 1970s, and in each television market across America basically three network affiliated television stations did in fact tell viewers what was news. In every town or city, large or small, almost exclusively white male anchor people told their audiences what was worthy of attention in their communities, using bite-sized chunks of information neatly conveyed at predetermined times—usually 6 p.m. and 11 p.m.—each evening. Between those times, came news of far-off lands—we used to call it foreign or world news, usually at 6:30 p.m. only and usually with someone named Walter, Chet, or David at the helm.

We called this the network news, and its 30-minute format (only half the 60 minutes given to events close to home) implied that it was only half as worthy as what was going on in our backyards—the domain of fires, movies, and beer. And it made money. Lots of money. It was, after all, the only news that viewers could see in their living rooms, so the belief grew that it was the ONLY news.

Of course, such a narrow definition of news was limited to events that were perceived to affect our lives the most. For most purposes, that meant events that took place within the narrow geographical boundaries in which most Americans worked and lived their lives. It was reality according to the "Big Three," as CBS, NBC, ABC and their counterpart local affiliate stations were then called. Not only was news *what* we said it was, it was also *when* we said it was. Viewers were captives on two levels: they had to watch only what the prevailing media of the time chose to tell them, and they also had to watch at a prescribed time, twice a day, with no flexibility. Miss and it and your next chance to be informed, at least via television, was the next day.

No competition meant this singular vision of the world was safe and intact, both for news people and their audiences. And so it remained from television's beginnings in the 1950s until nearly three decades later. Today it is hard to conceive of a time when so many Americans had so few options for their news and information. News consumers were seemingly content with their ration of fires, movies, and beer twice each day.

Fast forward. The date: June 1, 1980. The place: Atlanta, Georgia. The flag of the United Nations flew alongside the U.S. and Georgia flags. The man once called a lunatic, who would one day be labeled a visionary, was about to open a new chapter in the history of communications. The date may fade, but the event was every bit as cataclysmic as Gutenberg's contribution to the printed word.

This "mad genius," this "crazy visionary" was, of course, Ted Turner. Whether Turner realized it or not, his 1980 launch of CNN was perhaps the single most important action taken toward changing how we define news, from the perspectives of both content and delivery. While originally calling his new enterprise "America's News Channel," Turner clearly had a larger ambition: to create an international news service that would expand the definition of news to include people and concerns beyond our rural and urban neighborhoods and national borders. Toward that end, he wrote in a staff memo:

> It is the policy that any person, event, etc. which is not part of the United States be referred to as international rather than foreign . . . the word foreign implies something unfamiliar and creates a perception of misunderstanding. In contrast international means "among nations" and promotes a sense of unity.[1]

Turner's vision was large; his budget, formidable. But neither could overcome an equally formidable reality: in 1980, only about

20 percent of American households had cable television. Of that number, Turner's news channel reached less than 2 million, and that meant it was impossible to make a profit.[2] While embracing cable and building on relationships with local operators, Turner's vision was supplemented by the burgeoning system of satellites now available to deliver CNN nationwide and worldwide.

Not overnight and not without growing pains, CNN eventually made dramatic, definitive and lasting contributions to how news is conceived, produced and delivered. First, it significantly changed the concept of what is news. No longer is news what "we" tell "them" it is. No longer does it relate only to events within our direct sphere of experience or within the narrow geographic boundaries in which most Americans live. No longer does news exist only at certain times of the day or night, when the news providers, the networks and local stations decide to air it.

Turner's concept is "news on demand," around the clock, 24 hours, seven days. Nothing could have been more radical for nor more suited to its time, for "the growth of the global economy, coupled with CNN's readily available news programming, made the push to distribute CNN internationally an obvious business strategy for Turner."[3]

Turner's vision has, of course, been transformed into the news consumer's imperative. Not just viewers of television news but newspaper readers as well have since taken the reins in demanding immediate information wherever they are and whenever they want it. This has created a marketplace for international news that has broadened the reach of news organizations into nations where they might never have otherwise expanded.

While CNN is far from the only 24-hour, all-news network in the 21st-century media marketplace, in many ways it established the rules of operation within that marketplace. Part I of this work examines the trend toward the marketing of international news both in the United States and around the world, beginning with Don Flournoy's "Courage, Competition, and Credibility: The CNN International Standard." This thorough, critical study examines the network's legacy in light of those standards it helped set for competition in the global news marketplace. Professor Flournoy, widely recognized as the leading scholar in documenting CNN's strategy for success in uniting journalistic excellence with business acumen, argues that the standard is still in evolution even as the Turner corporation forms new partnerships domestically and internationally.

Next, as a companion piece to Professor Flournoy's study, are the candid comments of CNN Chairman, President and Chief Executive Officer Tom Johnson in a conversation that took place soon after the AOL–Time-Warner merger in early 2000. I was able to interview the CNN CEO for close to an hour, and the result is a look behind the scenes at the network's origins and influence from the perspective of the man chiefly responsible for the news coverage seen daily by a potential audience of a half billion viewers.

Balancing this view of CNN's niche in global news marketing is the perspective of a print journalist from the Associated Press, Kevin Noblet. AP's deputy international editor in New York and a former international correspondent, Mr. Noblet shares his view of the challenge of making news both interesting and understandable to a global audience. In the process we learn from a practitioner and editorial decision maker that much of what is marketed as news both here and around the globe is dependent upon a number of factors, not the least of which is a clear sense of audience.

The audience may be global, but the argument from János Horvát is that the perspective is clearly American. In "American News, Global Audience," Horvát, a media consultant, critic, and scholar in his native Hungary, suggests that the complex task of understanding the rest of the world is a challenge for which American journalists are ill-suited, by both education and inclination. Closing Part I, his perspective is both critical and diagnostic. He points out that before World War II, "American journalism could afford to be isolated, to cater to a public with little interest in world affairs." Horvát writes that since then, however, U.S. journalism has gone global and "can no longer cater to a public that is geographically, politically, and philosophically detached from the rest of the world." He suggests that realizing this fact could help better position global news in a marketplace that values balance, not distortion.

If Horvát argues that cultural values are a large part of how we perceive and present world events to others, Corey Flintoff's piece, "The Role of Cultural Values in Determining What is News," is a closer examination of how one specific story that captured the world's imagination toward the end of the 20th century reveals much about who we are as a society. The story of the president and the intern—Bill Clinton and Monica Lewinsky—eclipsed virtually all news, national and international, in the spring of 1996. Flintoff, an award-winning anchor of National Public Radio's "All Things Considered," asks some critical questions about our priorities in light of the kinds of important stories that were displaced by what some might consider the trivial public pursuit of a private issue.

The potential for displacement of a smaller nation's indigenous news and the cultural impact of that trend is the primary theme of Paul Norris' "News Through Alien Filters." Norris, a veteran New Zealand broadcaster and educator, surveys the gamut of news media in his native country—newspapers, magazines, radio, television, and the Internet—in order to distinguish the myriad ways in which the dissemination of news may become subject to an alien filter. The pervasive influence of American news is felt both in content and style of presentation, but so is the use of the preferred BBC reports. Norris' perspective is a strong reminder that globally distributed news can, but doesn't have to, overpower a small nation's cultural self-identity.

By contrast, Hussein Amin points out that national news policies in his native country safeguard against such cultural intrusion in "Visual Information in Egyptian Television News." "Egyptian television national news policies," he writes, "reinforce cultural and national traditional values; any visual content that causes social confusion or denounces the traditions of Egyptian society is forbidden." The mediating influence of such policies minimizes the opportunity for the kind of cultural impact imported news can have on Arab society. Even so, as Dr. Amin points out, his homeland is not fully immune to changes in how news is presented. The influence of global news delivered via satellite is felt in a new emphasis on the visual elements of a story, including the increasing use of video and graphics in a medium that once consisted only of the spoken word.

The spoken word via radio news took a major step forward through a bold experiment the BBC and American Public Radio undertook in 1995. The result, titled "The World," attempted to bring together the cultures not only of two nations but of two very different news traditions: the staid, some might say stodgy, BBC style with the less formal, street-savvy style of American radio. The program's U.S. anchor, Tony Kahn, takes us on a journey into the making of a program that reaches more than a million listeners through 110 stations in America, Europe, and parts of Africa. Innovative and exciting, "The World" is a pioneering example of emerging partnerships in the global news business. Kahn's "News on a Global Frequency: Fusing Contrasting Cultures in Radio News" is a fascinating look behind the scenes at how news decisions are made from two very different editorial perspectives.

In March 2000, Ted Koppel brought a perspective gained from 17 years as an international correspondent for ABC to the Red Smith Lecture in Journalism at Notre Dame University. Koppel, who before becoming anchor of ABC's "Nightline," reported from Vietnam, Latin America, Asia, and the Middle East, told his student audience that current trends in journalism make the basic reporting process both easier and harder. In "Journalism: It's as Easy as ABC," he stresses that faster communication systems have led international correspondents to adapt their entire approach to getting and delivering the story to viewers back home.

Stacy Sullivan's "New Wars, New Correspondents," echoes the theme that a new, interdependent world requires a new approach to the role and responsibilities of international correspondents. Sullivan's self-journey leads the reader to a greater understanding of how and why news from faraway places has become more relevant to Americans. Like Koppel, she spent years in the reporting trenches abroad; unlike him, Sullivan is a freelance reporter. From this very different perspective, she is critical of hiring practices in foreign news bureaus. Having much of our international news reported by what Sullivan calls "younger and thus cheaper journalists" with little regional expertise or overseas experience raises provocative questions about the quality of the coverage the audience receives.

Lending validation to Sullivan's argument is a former international correspondent and editor of the *Los Angeles Times*. Alvin Shuster addresses the news media's priorities when covering news from around the globe in light of audience interest and the economics of sending and housing news people in far-off places. "Global News, Changing Views" provides an excellent summary of how print and broadcast media have been steadily downsizing their foreign bureaus since the collapse of communism. In an attempt to shed light on the impact of cutbacks and recession on global news coverage toward the end of the 20th century, Shuster's study surveys news media trends in Asia, Africa and Latin America.

Agreeing with Shuster that the collapse of the Soviet Union has had a profound effect on global news coverage, Richard Lambert presents an alternative perspective on the international correspondent's role. Rather than seeing cutbacks and lack of audience interest as the primary determinants of the size and scope of international news bureaus, Lambert, an editor of Britain's *Financial Times,* sees an increased emphasis on reporting that integrates business, politics and culture. His position is that while the old model of international news reporting is in decline, the global economy has spurred a new model based on correspondents who specialize in business news.

Building on the origins, cultural values and process of global news, Part IV looks at the future of the news media in a world of advanced technology and audience niches. A former broadcaster, who was among the first African-American television news directors in America, Michael McKinley leads the way with an insightful look at how news organizations are underutilizing the Internet. According to McKinley, news organizations face a critical decision: do they remain focused on an old concept of news that revolves around public service, or do they embrace the new technology, which may mean adopting an entirely different concept of journalism?

New technology has brought new questions regarding the role of ethics in a world of instant access to news via satellites and the Internet. I argue in "Rapid Access and the News Consumer: Ethical Aspects of Today's Technology," that the future of global news depends more than ever on an adherence to traditional ethical standards. Tracing the rise of rapid global communications technology during the last 30 years, I suggest that journalists can overutilize technology by stressing content over context, process over perspective. Increased access to more sources of news doesn't automatically guarantee increased understanding.

As journalists in eastern Europe struggle to understand many of the concepts and processes central to the role of journalism in a free society, many U.S. journalists have found themselves teaching—and learning—in nations like Romania, Czechoslovakia and Hungary. Bailey Barash, a former award winning network news and documentary producer, has spent several years exploring the future of global news as it reveals itself in these former Soviet block nations. Her collaboration with Romanian journalist Ioana Avadani in "The Future of News in Eastern Europe: A Study of Promise and Potential" presents a fascinating look inside the development of global news on one of its last frontiers.

As systems continue to be developed for distributing news globally, an emerging concern for the future is that all people have access to the world of information available online. Allison Davis presents us with a firm reminder that the future of what we call global news may not be everyone's future. Dealing with issues of "information inequality" and its impact on people of color, Davis is a voice of consciousness and conscience in her insistence that global understanding is only possible if all people are included in the process. "Bridging the Digital Divide: Leading the Disenfranchised into the Information Age" presents a compelling case that the future of global news really belongs to people, not executives.

And that in many ways is the primary theme that weaves throughout all 16 of these perspectives on global news. While news professionals often disagree as to what is global news or how it is best delivered to an audience, the consensus emerging from among these authors is that the audience will decide the future. As one contributor to this book writes so succinctly, global news cannot be separated from the effects it has on its audience anymore than that audience's immediate reaction to a story can be overlooked. Especially on-line, that audience feedback can and probably will have an immediate impact on the direction the story takes from that point forward.

As we move toward a definition of global news, only one thing appears to be certain: the power to determine what information and how much information is important has shifted from the editorial desk to the consumer's mousepad. Anyone who has tracked the decline in readership and viewership for traditional news media has sensed this shift in the paradigm of power. News is no longer what "we" tell "them." Now it is what "they" tell "us." Perhaps part of our obligation is to listen.

Notes

1   Quoted in Don M. Flournoy and Robert K. Stewart. *CNN: Making News in the Global Market* (Luton, U.K.: University of Luton Press)
2   Ibid.
3   Ibid., 5–6.

PART I

Global News in the
International Marketplace

CHAPTER 1

Coverage, Competition and Credibility: The CNN International Standard

Don Flournoy

On December 31, 1999, Cable News Network (CNN) was well into its millennium coverage, a hundred hours of live programming originating from locations in every time zone. For days, CNN had been following the story of an Indian airliner taken over by Pakistani militants and flown to several airports about the Middle East. The plane had come to rest in Kandahar, Afghanistan. The hijackers were demanding release of Pakistani prisoners held in Indian jails in exchange for the safety of the airline passengers and crew. The militants on-board had guns and hand grenades, and one passenger had already been killed.

That was the day India conceded to the hijackers' demands and the Indian foreign minister arrived in Kandahar with the prisoners. The hijackers promptly exited the plane and disappeared with their colleagues into the interior of Afghanistan. Given the difficult conditions for news coverage, in which Afghanistan's Taliban regime had placed strict limits on news cameras in the vicinity of the airport, gathering news footage, especially live news, was almost impossible.

Don M. Flournoy is director of the Institute for Telecommunication Studies at Ohio University. He is the author of many articles on global news as well as U.S. media coverage of Canadian issues. He co-authored with Robert K. Stewart *CNN: Making News in the Global Market,* a work considered by many to be the definitive study of the network's development into the dominant news company in the international arena.

Fortunately for CNN, correspondent Nic Robertson and cameraman Todd Baxter had managed to bring to the scene a Toko unit, a backpack-sized store and forward digital converter, which allowed a video camera to be linked to CNN headquarters in Atlanta via satellite by means of a special mobile phone. Under normal operating procedures, this unit permits one minute of video to be digitized and transmitted at high quality over a period of 30 minutes. In the case of the hostage exchange, the unit was set to operate in real time in which only one of every six frames was transmitted. The pictures were dark and the motion was choppy, but these were the only live images out of Kandahar.

This event represents what CNN does best: successfully covering difficult breaking news stories and bringing them to the world live as they happen. CNN cut into its millennium celebration programming knowing that its global audience would want to be present at the next dramatic episode in the Indian hijacking drama, or whatever other story was unfolding anywhere on the planet. And it is to gain access to this type of timely news footage that broadcast, cable and satellite news stations, including stations in India and Pakistan, are eager to enter into partnerships with CNN.

Turner's CNN

Cable News Network (CNN) celebrated its 20th anniversary on June 1, 2000. An enterprise of Turner Broadcasting System of Atlanta, Ga., CNN began business in 1980 to test the U.S. market for a 24-hour news channel. The new CNN satellite service was targeted at the approximately 20 percent of U.S. TV households wired to cable—more than a million potential viewers. Today, CNN programming is within reach of a billion people worldwide and has more daily viewers outside the United States than within.

The CNN Newsgroup hosts almost a dozen news channels and a wholesale news service called CNN Newsource that sells video news to some 600 stations and affiliates worldwide. The affiliates also generate locally developing news that can be fed by satellite to Atlanta or to one of CNN's regional bureaus from almost every country. CNN's global growth has led to an increase in the number of international news bureaus to 37 (27 of which are in international locations) and news staff of more than 4,000. Much of CNN's growth has taken place at a time when almost all the over-the-air networks, in the United States and elsewhere, are slashing budgets for international news gathering.

What is the secret to CNN's success? The CNN brand is virtually synonymous with news and the standard to which many local, national and international news organizations aspire. The public consistently turns to the channel when they want to know what is going on, especially for breaking news. CNN is a profit center for Time Warner Inc. A key is the company's out-front competitiveness, which sets the pace for others. CNN has been willing to invest in and employ the latest in advanced technologies, which give it speed and extend its reach, and the company has been quite clever at developing local partnerships that ensure near-universal access to news and a broad market for its products.

CNN Coverage

CNN employs a flexible physical infrastructure and approach to personnel deployment that enables it to gather and report the news more efficiently than any other news network. CNN's global position today must be credited to its founder, Ted Turner, whose personal energies and financial resources were committed to the idea that gathering and distributing the news on a 24-hour basis could be a profitable business. It was Turner who pushed to take CNN into the international arena. The reputation of CNN as a reliable and credible news source for the rest of the world has been hard won, but not yet assured, something the company worries about and works on earning every day.

CNN built its reputation for going anywhere and staying as long as it takes to cover a story. This was demonstrated in its coverage of the Tiananmen Square confrontations in Beijing in 1989, its presence during the Persian Gulf War and in the dissolution of Yugoslavia and the Soviet Union, as well as in the fact that CNN stayed with those stories in the aftermath. CNN gave near-continuous coverage of the impeachment of President Bill Clinton (some say too much coverage), of the NATO action against Serbia and of year 2000 concerns around the world. Much of this news was live and unfiltered, much of it happened simultaneously with other important events, intensifying the challenge of timely news gathering and distribution.

Satellites

Technologies are crucial to the news business, especially in international news operations. CNN absolutely depends on hardware to accomplish its work. From the beginning, satellite distribution was the vehicle Ted Turner used for giving his Atlanta-based UHF TV station a national presence in 1976, and again in 1980 with the launching of the 24-hour cable news service.

Satellites enabled Turner to be the first international broadcaster blanketing the globe using a mixture of Intelsat, Intersputnik, PanAmSat and regional satellite signals. CNN's international and national desks coordinate coverage with its bureaus, correspondents, affiliates and outside news sources, such as the video news services of Reuters (RTV) and Associated Press Television (now APTV), 24 hours a day. CNN's signature live coverage would not be possible without satellites, which have helped the company transmit live reports out of such places as Libya, the Soviet Union, Iraq, Somalia, Bosnia, Peru, Pakistan, Chechnya and, possibly CNN's most unique live shot, Pyongyang, North Korea.

CNN now employs a satellite system that covers six continents, reaching some 210 countries and territories, with potential access to a billion people every day. Even in countries where CNN is unavailable to people in their homes because of limited cable or satellite systems or political constraints—CNN International has come to be the prevailing choice of viewers in hotel rooms, government ministry offices and presidential palaces.

The satellite infrastructure that gives CNN its global coverage is now better integrated with landlines. According to satellites and circuits vice president Dick Tauber, rapid growth in fiber optics linking population centers around the world has given CNN access to greater communications capacity. Several of CNN's international bureaus use ISDN (high-capacity phone) lines offering satellite-quality audio. Reporters can now record voice tracks to be combined with images already on file at CNN Center, avoiding the high costs associated with satellite feeds. From places such as Beijing, where ISDN is not readily available, bureau personnel enter their audio reports into computers and send them via e-mail to Atlanta, where they can be covered with in-house pictures. By 2003, Tauber predicts that both satellites and landlines will be all-digital and seamlessly integrated, which will enable CNN to do more with faster turnaround at less cost.

CNN headquarters in Atlanta is itself being converted from an analog, tape-based facility to a digital server-based environment. This will permit incoming news, arriving in digital format, to be more quickly edited and made available to viewers via one or more of the company's many news outlets. Ultimately, CNN plans to interlink its domestic and international bureaus over a CNN all-digital, wide-area network.

In 1999, CNN entered into a $20 million contract with Sony and IBM for a comprehensive "media asset management" digital storage and processing system that will permit integration of archived content—which is predominantly analog—and new material being generated, all in near-real time. CNN's stated intention is to make the entire archive of CNN video available to the desktop of every news producer. According to CNN's chief information officer, Scott Teissler, the system will "allow all tapes to go away and all video will be accessible as files."[1]

The Internet

The Internet has taken on a larger role in news delivery direct-to-users. CNN Interactive works closely with the broadcast divisions to gather and report the news, speeding communications between Atlanta and company bureaus, affiliates and contributors and hyper-linking viewers to international affiliates through their intercon-nected Web pages.

The CNN Interactive (CNNi) unit was created in January 1995 and is CNN's fastest growing news division. Starting with a modest staff of six, by the end of 1996, 130 people were working in CNNi. Four years later, the number was more than 400. In 1995, no one at CNN was prepared to predict the ultimate impact of the Internet on the news business or on CNN. Even today, the network's managers are unsure where the Internet is going, but are devoting money, space and staff time to it to be certain CNN is on the journalistic and creative edge of this new medium, whatever form it takes.

CNN.com ranks second in the United States among news Web sites, with between 6 million and 7 million unique users stopping at the site each month. The AOL–Time Warner merger is expected to raise CNN's online profile among AOL subscribers, which number more than 21 million. CNN's president of newsgathering and inter-national networks, Eason Jordan, told Multichannel News he thought "convergent technologies" were going to change CNN's game. "As we experience revolutionary changes, such as the conver-gence of content and technology on televisions, the Internet and devices such as mobile phones, we plan to be at the forefront of the efforts that bring people all over the world the most detailed news possible in their own languages."[2]

CNN Interactive produces 11 Web sites. In addition to *CNN.com, CNNfn.com* is a financial news and information site that is the companion site to *CNNfn,* the financial news network; *allpolitics.com* is a U.S. political news site produced in conjunction with *Time* magazine; My CNN is a customized news site; and there are seven international sites. The company also hosts *CNNSI.com,* a joint venture between CNN and Sports Illustrated, which is the home of *Sports Illustrated on the Web* and the sports site featured on *CNN.com.*

"The CNN Web sites are an integral part of the mission of the CNN News Group," Scott Woelfel, president of CNN Interactive, said in an April 2000 interview. "Our goal is to deliver news and information to anyone, at any time in the manner most convenient to that person. In a single day, the most convenient outlet may range from television to a desktop computer to a mobile phone. Our division is flexible and savvy, enabling us to keep pace with technology as it emerges."[3]

The bandwidth available to the vast majority of Internet users accessing the Internet via dial-up telephone lines in the new millennium is still too limited to carry heavily illustrated text graphic packages, audio or video. But higher speed transmission using newly upgraded cable, telephone, wireless and satellite channels promises to give new life to Internet-based programming. Among the attractive features of the Internet for news distributors such as CNN are its global reach, the prospect for real-time interactive communications, news on demand and reasonably economical access.

What worried the news media early on, given the fact that individuals and groups anywhere in the world could set up their own news sites, was that unfiltered information could be accessed and exchanged without an intermediary. If citizens could collect and distribute their own news, who would authenticate the news and what would be the need for the news organizations? With thousands, even millions, of Web pages hosting news-type material of all sorts appearing on the Net, the congestion and clutter alone is sending much of the viewing public back to their old reliable news sources, to find out what they should pay attention to.

The news organizations quickly figured out that the Web enabled them to offer their news with greater detail, personalized and on demand. CNN Interactive found that it was able to do more regional news. Local issues that did not merit carriage on the television networks could be included on local Web sites. *CNN.com* users were freer to choose what they wished to see and when.

An example is CNN's *www.cnn.com/asianow,* which has become a kind of one-stop shop for Asian news. With content from CNN sources and the weekly magazines *Time* and *Asiaweek,* all members of the Time Warner Inc. family, the *Asianow* Web site has become an important additional news source for what is going on within the region. The site subdivides news by region within Asia and presents special interest sections on business news, travel, entertainment, sports and weather.

Front-page headlines from across the region are given, as are news clips from the rest of the world with relevance to Asia. Audio feeds, links to *Asiaweek* and *Time* magazines and to news archives and a search function are included on this site. The *Asianow* site gets about 10 million hits per month.[4]

"With the strength of our content, we can create our own Web pages and people will find us," TBS president for Latin America, Jon Petrovich, told *IC* (*International Cable*) magazine in May 1999. "We're creating Web sites in Spanish, Portuguese, Finnish, Swedish, German and we're about to do Danish. The sites offer international and local news, weather, linkage to our affiliates—that's how we build business."[5]

Woelfel agrees. "We believe that CNN's worldwide reputation for providing accurate, timely news makes it the perfect Web site brand extension. Our broadcast divisions already have significant resources in place to gather and report the news worldwide, so it makes sense for us to expand our international Web presence." He noted that CNN Interactive would be launching additional international sites, each in a local language with a focus on news that is of particular interest to that area.

Both satellites and computer networks represent ways to overcome the physical limitations of the terrestrial broadcast signal. Each of these technologies permits news to be exchanged quickly, leapfrogging cultural boundaries and border checkpoints with relative ease.

CNN's Competitiveness

Once CNN opened for business, Ted Turner lost no time building on the 24-hour news concept. By 1981, he had added CNN Headline News to his offerings, and in 1982 he added CNN Radio, each of which drew upon the same news sources but reached a slightly different audience. The list of CNN news networks, which complement the TBS entertainment networks, has continued to grow (see Table 1.1).

In recent years, the company has joined forces with local broadcasters to create CNN-branded programming in the vernacular in Germany (CNN Deutschland), Spain (CNN+) and Turkey (CNNTurk). Non–English language Web sites produced by CNN Interactive include *CNNBrasil.com; CNNenEspanol.com; CNNItalia.it;* Svenska CNN; CNN Norge; CNN Denmark and the latest *CNN.co.jp,* launched in Tokyo in April 2000.

Table 1.1. CNN News Networks

Network	Launch Year
CNN	1980
CNN Headline News	1981
CNN Radio	1982
CNN International	1985
CNN World Report news exchange	1987
CNN Newsource	1987
Noticiero Telemundo–CNN	1988
CNN Radio Noticias	1988
CNN Airport Network	1992
CNN Interactive (*CNN.com*)	1995
CNN fn (Financial News)	1996
CNN SI (Sports Illustrated)	1996
CNN En Espanol	1997

"If we didn't have convergence on our doorstep already, along comes AOL," says president and managing editor for CNN International, Chris Cramer. With the Internet, CNN acquired a totally new series of highways on which CNN programming could be carried. "Our strategy before AOL came along—and certainly since AOL came along—has been to develop multiple vernacular Web site versions of CNN and to develop partnerships where wireless application protocol can be used to get CNN onto Nokia phones or any other application available to us, some of which have not yet been invented."[6]

"We have the mothership, which is CNN International; we have the regionalized versions of CNN International; we have the vernacular versions of CNN, and we now have the foreign language Web sites," Cramer notes. "Now we have a series of entirely connected information platforms which carry, perpetuate and grow the CNN brand worldwide."[7] He said CNN would need all of these to sustain a profitable business.

What makes CNN so efficient is that it can afford the cost of comprehensive news coverage because it can repurpose and reuse the same news material on more than one network, keeping the per-story cost low in comparison with other less well-diversified news networks. CNN maintains a highly centralized news-gathering operation whose mandate is to cover all the news that can be managed physically and financially, without regard to a particular audience that will receive the news or network on which the news will ultimately appear. Editors representing the various networks, including radio and the dot-com sites, build their rundowns from the collected news as it becomes available. Footage is archived so that pictures collected at one point in time can be quickly retrieved from the database for an entirely different purpose.

As an illustration, the Nic Robertson report from Afghanistan aired on CNN/USA, CNN International, CNN Headline News and CNN Financial Network, and the audio was used on CNN Radio. (Note that the story did not air on CNN Airport Network because CNN has a policy of not airing stories related to airline disasters on that channel.) The story was translated into Spanish for

CNN En Espanol, CNN Radio Noticias and CNN+; into Turkish for CNN Turk; and into German for CNN Deutschland. The report was streamed onto *CNN.com,* where the text was translated into a half dozen languages, and the report was sent out with, and without, the reporter audio track to more than 600 affiliates worldwide who pay CNN for the rights to their video. That same material was archived in the CNN Library for future CNN usage and Library tape sales. The efficiency comes from taking reports of a single news event and using them (read: selling them) over and over again.

Parisa Khosravi is vice president for international news coverage and managing editor of the International Desk. Her job is to see that CNN is on top of what happens outside North America, a responsibility managed centrally from Atlanta. This work involves "sending our people around to different parts of the world to cover breaking news and seeing that the news is covered from bureaus where our people already are. We of course have access to wire services and video news agencies and our many affiliates. It is the combination of all these resources that keeps the international desk very competitive."[8]

"We give a lot of autonomy to our bureaus," Khosravi added. "We expect them to be telling us what's happening in their beat. If it comes to deciding between two stories or moving correspondents and crews around, headquarters then makes that decision."[9] The International Desk is staffed 24 hours every day, which Khosravi perceives to be the most efficient way of communicating without adding unnecessary layers of approval.

"We are accessible to our people all the time," she says. For each shift, a certain editor is assigned a region each day. The assignment editors are communicating directly with the people in the field. As stories develop, the editors are also the liaison between the Desk and the producers of the various networks. "If someone on this end has a question, they go to that editor. If someone on that end has a question, they go to that editor," Khosravi explains. "That's what keeps us competitive and makes sure we are on the first flight and not waiting two or three hours for a decision."

Corporate Strategy

Ted Turner moved quickly to build relationships with broadcasters and cablecasters abroad. His goal was to identify additional outlets for his programming and to gain quicker access to breaking news stories, even in difficult-to-access places. This was his business agenda, but Ted Turner was not the conventional entrepreneur. He also had a larger personal agenda.

"Nobody ever gave the Palestinians or the Arab side a voice. Not here in the United States anyway. They didn't have a voice," he told me and Robert Stewart in a 1996 interview. "I read about the non-aligned nations griping about the fact that the Western news agencies controlled the flow of information around the world, giving a very biased impression about the world. The only time that news about India gets into the international media is when there's something like Bhopal (a toxic gas leak which virtually wiped out an entire village). That's absolutely true. It's outrageous."[10]

Turner looked for ways to give voice to voiceless people around the world and had a strong interest in the environment. He was passionate about nuclear disarmament and worked to bring an end to the Cold War. He established the Goodwill Games, promoting sports competition between Western countries and the countries affiliated with the Soviet Union, and created the Captain Planet series, an environmentally aware cartoon that featured multiethnic players. The creation of CNN, the rapid build-out of its international networks and the establishment of the CNN World Report newscast and news exchange were business ventures but they were also instruments of social change.

"I basically was trying to use the World Report and CNN and my power as someone who had some influence in the media to make the world a little better place, to try and improve understanding and goodwill around the world," Turner said.[11]

CNN World Report stands as perhaps the most dramatic and lasting of Ted Turner's diplomatic overtures in the international arena. In 1987, Turner asked his former Moscow bureau chief Stuart

Loory to invite every public and private news broadcaster in the world to participate with CNN in a radically different type of global newscast.

CNN World Report offered the opportunity for local broadcasters to submit a news report in English each week on a topic of their choice for use in a weekly newscast that was to broadcast on CNN/USA and CNN International. No money exchanged hands. Instead, broadcasters were given rights to air the contents of the program on their own channels. CNN agreed not to censor or edit the news submitted.

The international news community answered the call, slowly at first but eventually to include more than 200 news stations representing more than 140 countries. By the 10th anniversary of the launch of the World Report newscast and international news exchange in October 1997, some 20,000 news stories had been aired. Many of these reports were coming from countries rarely appearing in the news, covering breaking news, culture, human interest, sports and other topics.

"It is the philosophy of CNN World Report to be as inclusive as possible," Stuart Loory told a 1989 meeting of contributors which the author attended. "We are trying to create a true marketplace of viewpoints and perspectives on the news from around the world."[12] In this respect, the World Report program was quite unique. For the first time, news was intentionally not being collected and aired from a single point of view.

Turner wasn't content with news stations just sharing local news, however. He wanted newspeople to come to know one another, to share ideas and engage more global issues. This is why, in the second year after the launch of the World Report newscast and news exchange, Turner began inviting participating journalists to join him, along with CNN executives and staff, in meetings in Atlanta. The result was that news organizations from South Africa, Iraq, Vietnam, the Soviet Union and Greek and Turkish Cyprus, about 80 countries overall, sent representatives. Even competitor BBC showed up. At these annual gatherings, World Report contributors heard from world news makers, including U.N. director generals, presidents and prime ministers, whom Turner brought to Atlanta via satellite or in person, to address the important and timely topics of the day.

In a 1996 interview, Turner explained, "The World Report was to let the whole world be heard. To open up the whole world. Before the World Report, before CNN, (information flow) was like the spokes of a wheel, where everything was from the United States out and the United States back. That's all the information we ever got."[13]

It soon became clear that World Report was not just an act of do-goodism. CNN badly needed World Report for its international expansion. It needed to gain access to all countries for news coverage and to market its products. Many World Report contributors became paying affiliates and partners using Turner news and other programming on their stations. And when news broke in Iraq, Cuba, China, Libya—countries typically difficult for U.S. news organizations to work in—the friendly relationship with local journalists gave CNN unprecedented access.

Equally important, World Report had a role to play in the CNN corporate and organizational culture, helping to ensure that those representing CNN had the skills to successfully work in diverse cultural regions and societies.

Regionalization

Eason Jordan holds responsibility for CNN's news-gathering and international networks. It was he who hired CNN International managing editor Chris Cramer away from the BBC in 1996 to further internationalize CNN and ensure its competitive position in the global news market.

In 1996, CNN was acutely aware that it was facing a competitive marketplace that had not existed in the early years of CNN and CNN International. It was in that year that Eason Jordan hired Chris Cramer away from the BBC. In his position as CNN International managing editor, Cramer was given the mandate to further internationalize CNN and ensure its competitive position in the global news market. "There are a lot of things we must do—and will do—to not only maintain but widen the competitive lead we have. One of the things we are doing is regionalization," Jordan said at the time. "We are embarked on a path of simultaneously sending out separately-produced program strands to separate parts of the world. So while Asia might wake up to programming presented from Asia for Asians, at that same time Europe, Africa, Latin America and the Middle East will perhaps be seeing different programming."[14]

Shortly afterward, in a concept paper entitled "CNNI-Beyond 2000," Chris Cramer outlined strategies for developing new program formats and lengths, regionalizing CNN's international news services to provide more focus and relevance and creating specific programming for the Asian, European and Latin markets. The competitor he was most focused on was BBC World Service Television, because it was closest to CNN in terms of news product, but he was also keeping an eye on the various international channels of NBC, the Asia Business News, Euronews and Rupert Murdoch's News Corp. ventures around the world.

"If we are to maintain our carriage and influence in Europe and develop our carriage and influence in Asia, we've got to regionalize," Cramer said. "What we've got to do is to start producing tailored programming for individual regions."[15] The strategy was to start producing back-to-back parallel programming, part of it out of Atlanta, part of it out of the regions. Cramer noted that CNN International was already transmitting globally on 15 satellites using four distinct regional feeds.

A few months into the new millennium, Cramer was asked to comment on the changes made. "What's changed is a very rapid repositioning, if you like a reinvention of ourselves overseas." The last four years had been spent executing the Beyond 2000 strategy. The vast majority of CNN's international audience, Cramer quickly found, had only English as a second or third language and were watching from home, not from hotels. Few of the potential audience were American. "Not that (Americans) are not important to us but they are only one percent these days. So the entire constituency, the entire tapestry of eyeballs, had changed," he said.[16]

For Europe in particular, there was a massive rejection of U.S. programming, with the possible exception of movies. Cramer found this to be especially true of U.S. talk shows and current affairs/public affairs programming. CNN International's response was to invest heavily in programming produced out of Europe and out of Asia for four regionally focused international channels. A fifth channel, an English language channel out of South Asia targeted principally at India and Pakistan, was launched in July 2000.

Cramer told the *Times of India* that Indian audiences would continue to get CNN International news but through regional eyes with a regional flavor. "India, Pakistan, Sri Lanka, Afghanistan and Bangladesh will be able to see a different version of CNN. It will be distinctively different; it will have its own identity. Though it will still be a traditional news-breaking channel. There will be new faces, new voices and new coverage specifically customized for this part of the world.[17]

When Cramer reported to duty at CNN, about 60 percent to 70 percent of the programming was exported from the U.S. channel. By mid-year 2000, a majority was regionalized programming being produced outside of North America, Cramer told the author. "A whole bunch of programming is produced out of Atlanta, but about 75 hours a week are produced out of London and Hong Kong." He calculated that "nine out of 10 of our programs are produced for the international audience, not for the U.S. domestic audience. Only one of 10 programs seen on CNN/USA are now seen on CNN International. That's a massive change."[18]

Diane Schneiderjohn is senior vice president for network distribution and affiliate relations for Turner in the Asia Pacific. CNN was one of the earliest entrants to the region, launched in 1993, and was carried in 29 countries, she said in 1999. "We position (CNN) as the world's news leader—not international news, not local, not regional. It's about knowing what's going on in the world. Although it's in English, since 1994 we've tried to make it a truly accepted regional source of news. We originate over 12 hours a week of Asia-based news and that's increasing. We also provide in-country broadcast training for CNN-affiliated videojournalists, including sending them to Atlanta."[19]

The 1999 European Media & Marketing Survey placed CNN International in the top position for pan-European news. The annual survey interviewed 34,000 people, including a sample of 10,000 company managers, in 16 countries. CNN International was shown to have drawn 11.7 million viewers monthly, Eurovision 8.9 million, BBC World 3.7 million, CNBC 3.2 million and Bloomberg 1.1 million.[20]

Global Competition

Chris Cramer's concerns about his former employer rolling out big competition for CNN have yet to materialize. The competition from the BBC, News Corp., NBC and Bloomberg is mostly regional, competitive in some regions and not in others.

The television version of the highly acclaimed radio program "BBC World Service" was launched in 1991. BBC World Service Television, now called BBC World, is a news and entertainment channel with no government funding. The ability to mix into its news-programming world-class documentaries and features gives BBC a powerful international news schedule. BBC radio journalists are on-call in almost every country. Nevertheless, the fact that World Service Television is a project of public broadcasting in the United Kingdom that can expect no help from the British taxpayer yet must maintain a quality service equal to the name of the BBC is a major constraint.

BBC World's market-by-market approach to channel development has meant that it must find commercial partners in each region where it chooses to do business, relying on the BBC brand name and product to build a local audience. BBC World began in Asia as part of a package of Hong Kong-based StarTV programs. StarTV's signal was carried on the north beam of the Asiasat satellite, which covered Japan, Korea and much of China. When StarTV was purchased by Rupert Murdoch's News Corp. in 1994, BBC World was removed from the package. The reason given was that the BBC had offended the People's Republic of China with unflattering news coverage. China was StarTV's most important customer. Murdoch had good reason for not wishing to displease the Chinese: There are a potential 1 billion viewers in China and Murdoch had in mind to offer a global news service of his own.

BBC World was working hard to get going on an Arabic TV service for the Middle East region in partnership with the Saudi-backed Orbit Communications Group in 1996, when it lost its sponsor as a result of stories deemed unfavorable to Saudi Arabia. Thus, BBC World was taken off its distribution channel over the Middle East.

In 1998, the BBC signed onto a $600 million joint venture with the U.S.-based cable network Discovery. The BBC serves as one of several program suppliers. North America is a highly attractive market, which could prove profitable for BBC World, but it is also the region where the competition is most intense. As a news competitor in the North American region, the BBC is not yet up to speed.

Chris Cramer is reluctant to speak of his competitors, especially so about his former employer. "BBC World has not developed in the way the people in the BBC would have wished, primarily because they have yet to break even. It has been difficult for them. They were late in the game," he told the author. He acknowledges the BBC as genuine competition in Europe. He says he faces CNBC "mostly in Asia but not really in Europe. I have Sky in Europe but it is really a UK-centric service. I have Euronews, which is a competitor of sorts. I have Bloomberg TV which is small but it is going into the vernacular with multiple foreign languages."[21]

U.S. Competition

On its home turf is where CNN faces its greatest competition for the moment. The CNN/USA audience share is challenged daily by the comprehensive news channels, such as MSNBC and Fox, and specialized news channels such as ESPN, E! Entertainment, Bloomberg, CNBC and the Weather Channel. The U.S. domestic channel has been CNN's principal profit center. CNN's reputation for high-quality international news coverage is important in maintaining its edge with U.S. audiences. With a relatively fixed number of cable news viewers—the U.S. cable universe is about 70 million of 100 million households—CNN/USA has reason to worry that the gains made by competitors will be at its expense.

NBC-owned CNBC dominates the business news field in the United States. MSNBC, NBC's cable venture with Microsoft, is running second in U.S. cable ratings to CNN (12.8 million homes compared to 22.6 million). As the number one news Web site, *MSNBC.com* poses *CNN.com's* greatest competitive challenge. NBC's strong content combined with the Microsoft Internet Explorer browser places MSNBC on the opening screens of PCs the world over.

At launch, MSNBC vice president and general manager Mark Hartington announced that his service would be different from CNN and that there was room for both. "They've been at it for 15 years. With 60 million homes they have a different universe, but we have the strength of NBC News and its big-name talent as well as the Microsoft tie, which gives us an enormous step into the Internet world." To succeed, MSNBC must bring new viewers to the service, not just take CNN viewers, he said.[22]

Rupert Murdoch's Fox News Channel, headquartered in New York, was launched in 1996. It is now running third place to CNN and MSNBC in the U.S. market but has shown impressive gains. Roger Ailes is Fox News chairman and CEO. When asked by *Electronic Media* whether Fox was at a disadvantage in covering such international stories as Kosovo, Ailes acknowledged that MSNBC "took a little blip on us because they were able to drag all of their crack network talent into the picture. I mean Tom Brokaw was showing up every now and then." As for CNN, "They have massive resources overseas. They actually did a better job than MS. MS went away in 10 days. Our struggle is more focused on CNN," Ailes said.[23] According to ratings by Paul Kagan Associates, Fox News and MSNBC took in about $82 million in gross advertising revenues in 1999. CNN and Headline News taken together brought in more than $460 million. CNN says it is less interested in the ratings numbers because it sells advertising based on the CNN brand name and the income profile of its audience. Its competitors say publicly that this is just a way of playing down the fact that CNN/USA is no longer the power that it once was.[24]

In late 1999, the U.S. broadcast networks ABC, CBS and Fox entered into a news pool arrangement called Network News Service (NNS) to be coordinated by the three network affiliate news-feed services: ABC's NewsOne, CBS' NewsPath and Fox's News Edge. Much of the content will originate from the local stations, with affiliates agreeing to waive their exclusivity rights except for in-market. NNS is a counter to CNN's Newsource, which has dominated the domestic news-feed business since 1987. With its agreements for exchanging video with stations in almost every major U.S. market, and its ability to collect international news from everywhere, Newsource has assured local stations a greater diversity of breaking news footage while reducing those affiliates' news-gathering costs.[25]

CNN has been in off-and-on negotiations with each of the U.S. broadcast networks, with the exception of Fox, to assume some or all of their international news gathering. The basis for most of these talks has been the extraordinary cost of maintaining overseas bureaus, but the fact that CNN has built such a reputation that it has been hard for local or national broadcasters to compete in the international arena is also considered.

When former CBS newscaster Walter Cronkite was serving as CNN anchor in October 1998, providing coverage of Sen. John

Glenn's return to space on the shuttle *Discovery,* CBS was reorganiz-
ing and had layed off 125 people from its news division. CBS had
initiated talks with CNN about merging their news operations.
Cronkite told reporters that it appeared to him that broadcast networks like CBS had already ceded daily news coverage to the
24-hour news channels, particularly to CNN. "It's gotten so that the
networks almost need CNN because they have cut back so much on
their foreign bureaus."[26]

CNN Credibility

No news organization will survive as a news leader without credibility. CNN has had some of its toughest critics in the international
arena.

Western Bias

One of the most persistent of complaints arising from international
viewers over the years charges that CNN is an American news service that happens to be distributed internationally. This was the case
in the beginning, CNN agrees, but the company insists that image
is out of date and no longer represents reality. When Ted Turner dedicated his Cable News Network in June 1980, he raised the flag of
the United Nations at the opening ceremonies to fly alongside the
flags of the United States and the state of Georgia. Turner says it was
an early interest of his to make CNN an international news service.

By the mid-1980s, Ted Turner had spent more than $70 million
keeping CNN and Headline News afloat. With the explosive growth
in international trade and interest in world events, however, Turner
saw a growing need for up-to-date information on a global basis.
The CNN domestic service had been available in Japan and Australia beginning in 1982, combining the CNN and Headline News
services, but in 1985 a separate international news channel was

launched. The challenge has been not only to gather the news from every part of the world but to present the news in a way that is interesting and credible to global viewers.

The CNN International news team consists of some 250 full-time staff outside the United States and 25 assignment editors on CNN's international assignment desk in Atlanta. One way CNN has attempted to ensure that its coverage of world events is not limited to an American view is to hire non-U.S. citizens and to favor among U.S. hires those with international experience and language. Eason Jordan points with pride to the "great diversity in our presenting staff, in our reporting staff and in our behind the camera staff."[27] He believes this diversity is reflected in CNN's programming and how it formats its networks.

Because CNN International's news is now being tailored to broad regions of the world, the news one sees in Asia is somewhat different from that seen in Europe or Latin America. Nor are the faces one sees on CNN International the same, either among the anchors or among the correspondents. Throughout the 1990s, CNN's news-gathering, news production and presentation staff have been hired to consciously reflect both a regional and an international perspective. CNN International anchors shows from London, Berlin and Hong Kong, in addition to the United States. Although it is true that all news gathering, whether domestic or international, continues to be managed centrally from Atlanta, at least 15 different nationalities are represented on CNN's international assignment desk in Atlanta, and those staff are watching for news in every region of the world.

Parisa Khosravi is quick to demonstrate that the international desk that she manages is international more than in name. "I am Iranian. Looking around me right now I see we have a Croatian, Serbian, Scott, Tajiki, German, Russian, South African, British, Ethiopian, Belgian. This is not by accident. It is very much intentional. Every time we have an opening we look for diversity, we look for uniqueness, the languages, the backgrounds, the sensitivity these editors can bring to the story."

"Obviously journalism comes first but these are all pluses. Yan Mei, who is from China, might see something in a story that I wouldn't. Because she is from there, she understands the culture. She will flag something down probably quicker than anybody. So we will be quicker doing that story, quicker paying attention to it. This also results in many exclusives. I myself got the (Iranian) President Khatami interview. We send our editors to the field to make a difference in cases like that."[28]

Hiring by CNN has been aimed at addressing questions of cultural diversity almost from the beginning. The reason is that in globally distributed news programs, language, frames of reference, comparisons, metaphors used and presumptions about what the audience already knows are always troublesome. Attempts at taking into account cultural histories of all potential viewers are inevitably going to fall short of what news producers would like, but CNN's assumption is that viewers will reward those channels that make an effort. This is one of the reasons the vernacular programs are proliferating in the regions and on *CNN.com.*

Foreign News

In a memo to all staff in March 1990, Ted Turner wrote the following: "It is the policy of TBS that any person, event, etc. which is not part of the United States be referred to as international rather than foreign. The word foreign implies something unfamiliar and creates a perception of misunderstanding. In contrast, international means 'among nations' and promotes a sense of unity."[29]

Ted Turner is on alert to language that refers to "them" and "us," words that divide people. He readily admits that he is not a journalist, but he is very aware that frames of reference depend on the perspective from which the person holding the camera sees the story. The angle taken on the story depends on who the writers and editors are—each of whom contributes a different perspective based on experience as well as cultural background. Following this approach, the managers at CNN operate on the assumption that the key to producing a newscast that is worthy of the name "international" lies in the hiring process, in the orientation of staff and in working closely as a production and news-gathering team in the field as well as in Atlanta.

CNN has a stylebook that the staff are expected to follow in making decisions about how to phrase things: how to title news-makers; elimination of any ethnocentric language, such as *our troops* when referring to U.S. forces or those of any nation and elimination of the word "foreign" except in official government titles. CNN staffers say the hard part is in the writing. The writer must visualize the audience and make assumptions about what viewers know.

Khosravi told the author, "In our bureaus, a good percentage of our staff, if not all, are nationals from those regions. This is done intentionally to ensure that we are true to the story. The story is written and packaged by our reporters in the field; it is not written here. It comes back here for script approval so that everything is balanced, fair, accurate and grammatical."[30]

News Judgment

Sometimes the staff get spread pretty thin. During the NATO campaign, while CNN satellite dishes were under bombardment in Belgrade, CNN maintained extensive coverage of the Israeli, Indonesian and South African elections. It had staff in Turkey covering the Ocalan trial, in India and Pakistan covering the flare-up in Kashmir, in China covering protests over the bombing of their Serbian Embassy and in Russia covering ongoing economic and political developments. Deciding what news to cover and how much to spend covering it inevitably becomes a judgment call.

Khosravi was asked how priorities are established, given the practice of collecting news without regard to where the story will be used. "If there is a breaking story, all hands are on that story. Finding and checking the facts as quickly as they can and seeing that we are very competitive. We are responsible for making sure the news is covered. That is our first priority."[31]

The CNN News Group consists of many channels, each with their own interests, she explained. When the Desk has the luxury of time, a reporter can be assigned to do a feature story, and there are a lot of enterprise and longer feature pieces produced for programs like Insight and Inside Africa and Inside Asia. But "the priority remains hard news, breaking news. I have no problem pulling a person off to be sure we are covering the news that day."[32]

Khosravi was asked about CNN guidelines for deciding what is covered and what is not. Given limited resources and the entire planet to cover, who gets left out of the news? She says the International Desk tries to give some attention to everyone. "Even if we do not have our own CNN reporters on the story, we are likely to have pictures. If not our own pictures, then agency pictures. With over 200 affiliates, we count on them to fill in for us. It's very rare that we wouldn't at least have pictures of a story."[33]

But getting on the air is another matter, she said. It's up to the production side of the company to decide what goes into each show. "We are responsible for covering it and bringing it here to Atlanta. But what gets aired is not my decision. That's the decision of every single producer of every single hour of every network. It's a different person in every case. They are the ones making up the rundowns and deciding the priorities of their shows."

CNN must utilize its limited staff efficiently to produce a diverse and culturally sensitive schedule of programming, but the bottom line is that it must get the story straight.

The CNN production/news-gathering system is set up for speed. It employs the most advanced technologies and hires and trains personnel to respond quickly to news developments. But sometimes speed leads to mistakes. The result can be minor annoyances such as hoax callers getting on the air, as happened in the aftermath of the fatal car crash of Princess Diana, or in much more disturbing instances such as Tailwind and the handling of the Richard Jewel case.

During the summer 1996 Olympic competition, a bombing occurred in the Olympic Park adjacent to the CNN complex in Atlanta. Under pressure to be first with a story in its own city, and using a local newspaper as a source, CNN aired a story saying that security guard Richard Jewel was the FBI's leading suspect. Jewel was not charged and was later taken off the list of suspects. In June 1998, the debut broadcast of the network's Sunday night series, "News-Stand: CNN and Time," aired an 18-minute "Valley of Death" story alleging that the U.S. military used deadly nerve gas on American defectors in Laos during the Vietnam War. A month later, after much public criticism and an internal investigation, CNN retracted the story.

President and CEO of the CNN News Group Tom Johnson apologized to CNN's viewers for Tailwind. Insufficient evidence was present to support the allegation that sarin gas was used, Johnson said. "CNN alone bears responsibility for both the television reports and for the printed article in the June 15 issue of *Time* magazine. We acknowledge serious faults in the use of sources who provided News-Stand with the original reports." His investigation found that CNN's system of journalistic checks and balances, which had served CNN well in the past, had failed in this case. "We are taking vigorous steps to strengthen our internal procedures to assure that mistakes of this type do not occur in the future."[34]

"The nightmare that has occurred at CNN is what every news editor and journalist lives in dread of," CNBC senior vice president of business news Bruno Cohen told *Multichannel News* in response to CNN's retraction of the story.[35]

The Road Ahead

CNN continues to look for solutions for those times when news is slow. As a breaking-news network, its numbers go down when the world is at relative peace. According to an Associated Press report, CNN/USA audience ratings fell 31 percent in the first quarter of

2000 compared with the same period in 1999. The reasons given were that President Clinton's impeachment was in the news in 1999 and that, by 2000, rival CNBC was dominating business and financial news, capturing followers of the market that normally would have gone to CNN.[36]

Breaking news is still CNN's franchise, but the company has had to think hard about ways to smooth out the peaks and valleys (it says it prefers to raise the valleys) in its ratings. Internationally, CNN has been forced to make as many changes in its business strategy as it has in its editorial strategy. According to Chris Cramer, three streams of funding now support the channel: advertising, subscriptions and sponsorships. "To withstand some of the pressures of recessions in Asia and Latin America and not have to rely so heavily on U.S. advertisers, we now pick up advertising from the pan-region. That's where we do most of our business," he said. "We now produce for the back-half-hours of our news wheel regionalized programming which is not hard news programming. Some of this programming happens to attract extremely wealthy sponsors."[37]

Cramer explains that "sponsorship is when you have a client, such as the motor car manufacturer Volvo, who wishes to associate his name with a certain program, such as World Beat. The (music-oriented World Beat) program sounds good to them in terms of the demographic they are trying to attract, so they've entered into a multi-year multimillion dollar sponsorship." Another example is the weather service, which Cramer says is the most watched part of the International channel. "I relaunched the service a few months ago using international forecasters. We set up our own international weather center here (in Atlanta) and attracted Allianz, a huge pan-European insurance company. They sponsor our weather." These, he noted as examples of funding sources that had not existed in past years but, because of the CNN brand and regionalization, now bring in incremental revenues.[38]

The Internet is also high on the agenda. Traffic on the CNN Web sites almost doubled in 1999, the second year in a row to do so, according to CNN Interactive president Scott Woelfel. These sites served more than 6.7 billion page impressions in 1999, and 2000 proved to be a strong year as well. Woelfel said the Web sites have been profitable "in whole or part" since 1996 and generated millions of dollars in revenue in 1999. He notes, however, that CNN has chosen to defer short-term profits and reinvest revenue to ensure that the sites maintain their industry position.

Internet revenues are principally from advertising, according to Woelfel, although licensing is strong and e-commerce is growing. He expected future income generators to include subscriptions, merchandising and transactions. "Our brand helps us draw traffic. As CNN has been gathering and reporting news globally for almost 20 years, we are already established as a leader in disseminating information. Not only does this make for a very natural transition to the Internet, but CNN Interactive also has the luxury of drawing on the myriad of resources of both CNN and Time Warner publications, like *Time* magazine, one of the world's most respected magazines. This all offers depth and variety to our sites and gives us a strong edge on the competition."[39]

CNN International's revenues were estimated to approximate $200 million in 1999, the second largest profit center for the News Group. In the long term, international revenues are expected to outstrip domestic revenues, in part because viewer growth will be greater outside North America but also because the outlets for CNN product are increasing worldwide and new advertising dollars will be attached to much of that growth.

Notes

1. Glen Dickson, "CNN Invests in Digital Future," *Broadcasting & Cable,* 19 April 1999, 94.
2. Alan Waldman, "A Global Perspective," A Special Supplement to Multichannel News entitled Network to the World: CNN Turns 20, June 3, 2000, p. 15A.
3. Author interview with Scott Woelfel, April 2000.
4. Mansha Daswani, "Asia Web Review: Path Finders," *Cable.Satellite Asia,* January/February 2000, 22–23.
5. Alex Swan, "Programming: Controlling Churn the Turner Way," *IC,* May 1999, 64.

6. Author interview with Chris Cramer, April 2000.

7. Ibid.

8. Author interview with Parisa Khosravi, April 2000.

9. Ibid.

10. Don M. Flournoy and Robert K. Stewart, *CNN: Making News in the Global Market* (Luton, U.K.: John Libbey Media, 1997), 17.

11. Ibid.

12. Don M. Flournoy, *CNN World Report: Ted Turner's International News Coup* (London: John Libbey & Company, Ltd.), 25.

13. Author interview with Ted Turner, November 1996.

14. Author interview with Eason Jordan, November 1996.

15. Flournoy and Steward, *CNN,* 117.

16. Author interview with Chris Cramer, April 2000.

17. Gurmukh Singh, "Encounter with Chris Cramer: We're Not Ashamed About Making Profits," *Times of India,* 2 July 2000, 2.

18. Author interview with Chris Cramer, April 2000.

19. "Turner Broadcasting, Asia Pacific," *IC,* April 1999, 24.

20. Chris Forrester, "CNNI, CNBC Score High in Euro Survey," *Multichannel News,* 19 July 1999, 42.

21. Author interview with Chris Cramer, April 2000.

22. Flournoy and Stewart, *CNN,* 136.

23. Jon LaFayette, "Ailes Weighs in on Network Battling, War Overseas," *Electronic Media,* 21 June 1999, 16.

24. Deborah D. McAdams, "CNN Stood Up: Viewers Fail to Keep Their Appointments," *Broadcasting & Cable,* 13 December 1999, 45–46.

25. Steve McClellan, "Three Nets to Share News," *Broadcasting & Cable,* 3 January 2000, 12.

26. Linda Moss, "CNN Eyes Pacts with 'Big Three' Nets," *Multichannel News,* 19 October 1998, 30.

27. Author interview with Eason Jordan, November 1996.

28. Author interview with Parisa Khosravi, April 2000.

29. Flournoy and Stewart, *CNN,* 1.

30. Author interview with Parisa Khosravi, April 2000.

31. Ibid.

32. Ibid.

33. Ibid.

34. Linda Moss, "CNN Retracts Nerve-Gas Story," *Multichannel News,* 6 July 1998, 2.

35. Charles Paikert, "CNN Wrestles with 'Tailwind' Fallout," *Multichannel News,* 13 July 1998, 18.

36. David Bauder, "Fox News, MSNBC Take Different Lessons From CNN's Troubles," *Associated Press,* 19 April 2000, 1.

37. Author interview with Chris Cramer, April 2000.

38. Ibid.

39. Author interview with Scott Woelfel, April 2000.

CHAPTER 2

CNN: The Origins of the 24-Hour, International News Cycle

An Interview with Tom Johnson conducted by Tony Silvia

TS: I'd just like to talk to you a little bit about CNN in terms of the last 20 years and its beginnings, its origins; I know it's going to be a wide-ranging question, but could you comment on how you see the overall contribution to the advent of what we now refer to as "global news."

TJ: It has been said before, but I genuinely believe, that CNN revolutionized the entire news world. It brought 24-hour news to both those within the United States and around the world so that no longer did viewers or, for that matter, listeners as well, need to tune in at predetermined hours of the day—hours that had been set by producers, largely in New York—rather than at the convenience of the people who really needed news and information around the clock.

TS: In terms of some of the ways in which CNN has changed over the last 20 years, and there obviously are many, how is the network setting the pace for 24-hour news coverage today, in the year 2000?

Tom Johnson is chairman, president and CEO of CNN News Group. His career spans over four decades in broadcasting and print journalism, business and government. He joined CNN in 1990, following a distinguished career as deputy press secretary and executive assistant to President Lyndon Johnson, publisher of the *Dallas Times Herald* and the *Los Angeles Times* and vice chairman of Times Mirror Company. In 1999, the Radio Television News Directors Association honored him with the Paul White Award for excellence in journalism. The following interview, with Tony Silvia, took place in March 2000.

TJ: I divide the life of CNN into three waves—the first wave was from its creation in 1980 until basically the start of the war in the Gulf in 1990–91. That first wave was characterized by a maverick band of pioneers who were brought here by Ted Turner and who put CNN Headline News, and even CNN International, on the air. They did it against the weight of conventional wisdom; they did it with massive debt that was incurred. But it was this band of pioneers led by Ted and his vision and his absolute commitment to do it. So, that was really the pioneering stage, when the brand was established, the infrastructure was established, the distribution was established within the United States. The period 1990 to this past year, almost into 1999, was what I describe as the period of globalization. It was, in many ways, dramatically affected by the war in the Gulf. The war in the Gulf, and CNN's Gulf War coverage, served as a one billion-dollar promotional thrust. It enabled CNN to increase its distribution throughout the world. There were cable operators, and even broadcasters, all over the world who signed up to distribute CNN. It demonstrated that it could hold its own up against the BBC, ABC, CBS and NBC journalistically. It was an enormous forward thrust for a network that already had built itself within the United States, and it led, in this past decade, to the creation of many new bureaus, of many new sales offices, of extensive extensions of the brand into parts of the world that previously had no 24-hour news services.

TS: Has CNN affected other cultures significantly beyond the American culture?

TJ: I think it enabled many cultures to receive, for the first time, independent news—news that was not influenced by government broadcasters. Just take the former Soviet Union; CNN was distributed throughout the former Soviet Union, and the people were able to see not only what life was like outside the Soviet Union, but they were able to see CNN reporters from Moscow and other points as they reported on life within the then Soviet Union. We were there on the tanks with Boris Yeltsin when he helped to prevent the Ku that was trying to overthrow Gorbachev. We were there when he actually later attacked his own Russian Parliament building to try to keep the country from turning back to the hard-line communists. But that was true in many other parts of the world. It's seen in places—sometimes overtly, sometimes covertly—but it's seen in Cuba; it's seen in Iraq; it's seen in some limited way in North Korea; it's seen in hotels and a few places throughout China. In many ways, it propelled the historic coverage of the war in the Gulf and the rapid efforts to expand the networks. We created new channels for Germany—with German partners—that's our N-TV. A new channel for Spain with Spaniards; a new channel for Turkey, CNN-Turk; a new channel for Central and South America, CNN-Espanola; and built relationships with broadcasters around the world. If the first wave of CNN was building itself within the United States, and really competing effectively in that period, then the second wave was establishing itself and expanding throughout the world.

The third wave is the one that I think we're in today—I describe it as a new digital era; some would say it's a new interactive era, where we are converting CNN over from analog to digital. We are creating new services, new products, new content, and with the merger with AOL, will be on new platforms. In addition to the cable distribution and the direct-to-home distribution, we'll also be distributing through the Internet into your PCs and well beyond. This could very well be the most exciting era, I think, in the history of telecommunications, as we move to a time when every person with adequate economic means (that's a big distinction), but those who can access a computer—a terminal, a PC—will be able to get vast quantities of information. It's almost like having great libraries, or great newspapers, or great wire services, at their fingertips—health information, science information, you name it. The information is there whenever you wish to get it. Not only with wires, cable and telephone wires, but also with wireless. Many parts of the world today do not have wired systems. You'll see significant increases.

I think that we are into a period of almost a revolutionary period in telecommunications, and certainly as Turner went from the company that it was before its merger with Time Warner, then built even further in its relationships with Time Warner, like creating a new CNN Sports Illustrated channel, the new CNN and Time program, we now are into this period of the dot-com world in which the CNN brands can be extended even further through the new technology, the new distribution channels, whenever and wherever the public wants to get it. It not only will become the 24-hour news network, but it's almost going to become a minute-by-minute, on-demand service—on-demand news, on-demand weather, on-demand sports, and much, much more.

TS: It's interesting, because the new *Brill's Content,* or one of the later issues, I think it's the newest one, has a public survey, and CNN is ranked—in terms of approval rating by the public—higher than any other news source. That's despite the advent of MSNBC, and Fox and so forth. Clearly, your brand has stood the test of time. I'm not asking you to speak for Ted, but you talk with him all the time. Does he ever sit back and say that he kind of gave birth to these (I don't want to call them "imitators"), but he sort of gave birth to the networks that are now your competition?

TJ: Not only did Ted inspire the creation of the current CNN Turner services, but clearly the MSNBC and Fox news channels were established as a competitive response. They saw the enormous circulation growth, the revenue growth, the profitability growth, of this, and they were determined to try to get their share of it. Of course, Ted also would have owned what was the old Financial News Network, FNN, had his board permitted him to do it.

TS: CNN International is, in many ways, a different animal from CNN Domestic. Was that basically grown out of a need to, or perhaps a reaction from people in other countries who once suggested that CNN was not as global as it might seem on the surface? That it was still news distributed globally, but with an American bias—or, if not with an American bias, with an American point of view perhaps?

TJ: Well, the early criticism was valid. In the early years, what we put out was basically headline news to the world, with some international inserts going in. It was really only into the early '90s that we started creating channels specifically designed for the regions of the world. We now have a separate feed for Europe; a separate feed for Asia; a separate feed for Central and South America. I should just say that we believe that we have now built a worldwide, 24-hour English language service reaching virtually every country on the planet. But we've only just begun to reach the world in the other languages of the imported regions. It is our hope that we can, with local partners, expand in several other languages—not with translation services, but with locally originated news and information. One of our next targets is India, or a Hindi language channel.

TS: As we look ahead to this millennium, Tom, what do you see—not just within your own corporation, but across the spectrum of global communication—where do you see us? I know here's the multi-billion-dollar question, but where do you see us going? What's the next step?

TJ: Nobody can really project the future, long term. I see a world of multiple services, multiple languages, multiple technologies, but I also see a world in which there will be a few very high-quality services (by that I mean news channels and other services), and a large number of channels that may not be worthy of the audiences that we're trying to serve. Just as in the past, there have been tabloid newspaper wars in this country and in others. Going back to the days of William Randolph Hearst and others. I see a world where quality channels—quality products—will compete with lower-quality products. I think it's true in the entertainment side; it's true in the sports side; it's true in the news side. In the entertainment side you go from wonderful, wonderful work like Discovery, and A&E, and National GEO, and Biography, down to shows like we've seen this past weekend—"Who Wants to Marry a Multi-Millionaire?"—or real, R-rated shows, and soap operas, such as those in this country and novellas in other countries. In sports you'll go from the great sporting events to perhaps, what some would say, very, very unacceptable forms of athletics—this whole new form of athletics, extreme sports. Then on the news side, I think you will have high-quality news brands, but you'll also have the unedited, unchecked world. I do know this—Ted Turner, Gerry Levin, Steve Case are committed to operating very high-quality news and information services. Within Time Warner, that means the *Time* magazines; here it means CNN and the news channels. In our entertainment side, whether it's TBS or TNT or the Cartoon Channel, we are going to strive to really be the quality option—the quality path—in this new world. I saw the tabloid competition over the years, and the *New York Times* was able to rise in that New York market after it had really been attacked by tabloids for more than a hundred years. I saw it in the Los Angeles market, when not only Hearst, but others, competed there. I just believe that, ultimately, there will be a place for quality channels, and that's where we're trying to strategically position ourselves. That doesn't mean dull; that doesn't necessarily mean PBS, which is excellent quality, and maybe even at times the quality of the BBC—it means very, very high standards of accuracy, fairness and responsibility.

TS: That's not incompatible, I would take it in your view, with the growing age of what some would say and have said, is medium monopolization. There hasn't been a sacrifice in quality as fewer and fewer companies own more and more media outlets?

TJ: I believe that media critics and viewers will look very skeptically at these large media mergers and, if anything, with the regulatory authorities looking carefully at them, with the public looking very carefully at them, I think there's going to be a greater need— almost a demand—for these companies to produce and provide more quality than they might otherwise do. I think the spotlight is going to be more on these companies than it otherwise would be. I've heard enough about quality out of Steve Case, and I've now worked with Ted Turner and Gerry Levin for 10 years. I have confidence that we are going to serve the public interest. The old line that we all had back in my earlier broadcasting years—a real need to serve the public interest and to do it in a way that produces good programming and good profits.

TS: CBS News President Andrew Heyward recently said: "No matter where news goes, and no matter how it's delivered, whatever the delivery system, whoever the deliverers are, ultimately, content will be king." Do you agree?

TJ: I think content and distribution. You cannot achieve success without having distribution for the content. There have been a lot of very, very high-quality content products—newspapers, magazines—and I think that, particularly in this new world, that they are almost equally important in order to achieve success. You must get your service, your magazine, your newspaper, your cable channel to those who wish to receive it. We're going on the most powerful satellites in the world in order to reach the direct-to-home market. We're trying to go through the new technologies. It's very, very important. But clearly, what is most important to those of us who are journalists is the quality of the content. I would be dead in the water without high-quality distribution, too!

CHAPTER 3

Producing and Marketing News for the International Audience

Kevin Noblet

Putting together American news and delivering it to overseas audiences is a fascinating subject. Unfortunately, it's one that is not getting a lot of attention in the current debates over issues in global journalism. Most of the focus, when you think about international news, is concern over the shrinking news hole for international news. This results from what the marketers are telling publishers and the producers is the declining interest in news that comes from a great distance because of the increasing interest in locally oriented news: news you can use, news that "hits home." News, like politics, is local. I won't argue against it; I think any journalist who's been around sees that people like news that hits home. But I would argue that readers need to leave home occasionally if they are to, in a sense, redefine the changing world in which they—in which we all—live.

Early in my career, while working on a weekly newspaper in Connecticut, I got more cards and letters, more phone calls, more feedback by writing about a change in the town charter than on

As deputy business editor and former deputy international editor of The Associated Press (AP), Kevin Noblet helps direct the news agency's corps of more than 200 overseas reporters and shapes the AP's global news report from its headquarters in New York. A veteran journalist, Mr. Noblet has filed on-the-scene reports from many international locations, including Chile and Haiti. In addition, he teaches a course in global news reporting at Columbia University and has been a Freedom Forum Professional in Residence at Ohio University. The essay that follows is an edited transcript of a lecture given by Mr. Noblet at the University of Rhode Island in 1998.

almost any other story I've covered. The town was going to go from three selectmen to five selectmen; this was a big issue—an important issue for that community. I got feedback every week on my reporting. It wasn't that many years later that I was covering a change of government in Chile, where another dictatorship was giving way—finally after 16 years—to democracy. I didn't get any cards or letters about my coverage. I'm not sure there's anything wrong with that; I think we all like news that we feel touches us—that has some direct impact on us. But it is depressing when you're in a place like Haiti or Bosnia or . . . pick a place around the globe and think about the lack of feedback from the reporting there.

I was in Haiti for a couple of years. My title at that time was Caribbean Correspondent; I loved how it sounded, but it really meant that I would spend about nine months of the year in Port-au-Prince under an economic embargo with rationed electricity at the hotel. It wasn't really as glamorous as it sounded. The interest in Haiti ebbed and flowed in direct relation to how many Haitians were landing on the Florida beaches. When they weren't landing on our shores, the interest in Haiti subsided quickly. That can be a depressing aspect of covering international news. American news has a huge market, to use the crass commercial term, overseas. Around-the-world newspapers, radio and television can hardly get enough of it. They want it at all different levels—at the level of sports, the level of entertainment, the level of high politics and low politics; it's very exciting to see just how much space—even pages—the press in nations outside the United States will dedicate to the subject of America and American culture.

How do I know this? Where I work, in New York, shaping the AP's reports, we have two central functions on the international desk. One is to take the reports we receive from our 200+ correspondents overseas and shape them for delivery to our newspaper, radio and television members in America, all 1,550 of them on the newspaper side and 6,000 in the broadcast media. We also serve subscribers to the AP overseas—about 8,000 subscribers in 112 countries, not including the United States.

We deliver our news in five different languages—five languages other than English. And then, of course, any number of news outlets take our reports and translate them into other languages. That's just to let you know that we are very concerned, very mindful, of what they want and what they're looking for in places such as Jakarta, Johannesburg, Sri Lanka, New Delhi. They pay us in nice currencies, and we want to make them happy; we want to give them the information they want.

I asked one of the editors I work very closely with for an estimate of just how much of the total news market overseas American news represents. He estimated about 20–25 percent—that's in places such as Germany, Japan, South Africa. It makes me feel a little bit better about international news, because in these countries American news is international news and readers there want it. Newsapers dedicate lots of space to it; they have a feeling that it touches them and touches them directly.

I was trying to think about why—why is it that American news outlets are so insular and give so little space to international news, and why these other countries like it so much, not just American news, but also news from other parts of the world? It could be that in the histories of those countries, their citizens felt much more closely touched by events in other countries—a foreign invasion, an economic crisis that's brought on by events or policies of a country larger than themselves, or the intervention of a "superpower." In America, we sometimes have the luxury of feeling less touched by the events in other countries.

One axiom always to keep in mind with international news is that distance can be dangerous and allows people to create stereotypes, often false stereotypes, and can allow reporters to reinforce them with superficial or inaccurate reporting. We saw some of that overseas with the school shootings in Arkansas a few years back; the British tabloids, for instance, had a field day with the violent American culture—the gun culture.

They had a field day with the U.S. south—all of the stereotypes that we have about gun-toting, pick-up driving Americans. The

newspapers around the world loved that story, too. It was no accident that they loved it coming from Texas, which a large part of the
world has a certain image of and not necessarily a flattering one. You
can explain to them that northern states also have death penalties;
you can explain to them that men in Vermont also take their young
sons out hunting to learn how to use guns at an early age. But there's
a stereotype there, and the news, at its worst, is reinforcing those
stereotypes all the time.

We try to take seriously our role in not reinforcing those stereotypes by trying to include in our report stories designed to fill out
the picture by giving some much needed cultural perspective. That
can sometimes mean writing stories specifically with an international audience in mind, explaining a little bit about hunting and
guns. True, they still bring up the American gun culture and the
American hunting culture—but our intention should be to fill out
the total picture and provide some needed perspective. We fail our
readers if we let them simply think that school shootings happen
only in Arkansas, or only in the south. So, we try to make sure that
our stories go beyond superficial perceptions.

I think my desk is specially trained in this—or especially mindful of it—because of our 200+ correspondents overseas. As I have
said, distance is dangerous, and we sometimes see stories that our
people report from Japan about some Japanese idiosyncrasy. Just like
there's a market for those gun-toting Texans in the British tabloids,
there's a market in the States for those wacky Japanese stories. We
don't really like to cater to that, and because we see the tendency
toward it so much with our overseas reporters, we think it gives us
some expertise in trying to avoid the same problems with our American report headed overseas.

The Taliban in Afghanistan is one example of a phenomenon
that is sometimes oversimplified. I'm not expressing great sympathy
for its practices, especially those regarding women. People often
describe it as medieval, cruel, and maybe through a certain cultural
prism it is. On the other hand, I can recall asking one of our
reporters once, "Where do they get those head-to-toe veils overnight

from when they ordered that all women be dressed like that?" Our correspondent said, "Well, they got them out of their mothers' clothes closets." I said, "Well, wait a minute! You've been describing this as a practice brought back from medieval days." He said, "Well, no, it's really not medieval—it was like 20–30 years ago." It belied the notion that what they were doing was going back to the middle ages; they were going back to the 1950s. Our preconceptions were badly mistaken.

There's a lot of small editing that we have to carry out for an American report designed for overseas readers. The Monica Lewinsky story was huge around the world not so very long ago. Around that time, we carried a story out of Romania—Bucharest—because it had a Monica Lewinsky look-alike contest sponsored by the local town government. It was won by an 18-year-old woman; I don't believe you want all the details of her skit, but it showed an intimate familiarity with all the allegations. But, if you're sitting in New York with copy—there's a quote about "big hair," or "trailer trash"—you've got to explain this to readers in Tokyo. It's a pretty scary notion—"big hair"—what is it? These are little details that our editors have to deal with, and we run into them constantly with our international report to Japan or Poland or India. Every detail is important to an international reader, but every detail of a story steeped in American culture doesn't necessarily translate easily—or well.

There are other examples. O.J. Simpson is a prime one; in China citizens have never seen him run across an airport, let alone a football field, as one of our stories had to mention. There was no awareness of him as the sports star, but there was interest in the O.J. Simpson story—a long-running interest. At the core of that interest was racism: a topic that fascinates the rest of the world about the United States. And in many parts of the world they understand racism as the lynching of African Americans in Mississippi—because that's where they've read or heard it takes place. Again, we have a constant job trying to keep the picture clear on just what American racism is and where it is, beyond a specific physical location.

O.J. Simpson reminds me of sports. Sports is a nightmare for us because everybody's always talking about it; politicians are talking about it. People are always talking about "playing hardball," being in the "bottom of the ninth." These expressions don't translate to your audience in Budapest; you always have to fix those. Lou Gehrig's disease is only a disease in the United States. If you want to explain that to somebody overseas, you have to give it its proper name, and then put (comma), "which Americans refer to as Lou Gehrig."

Movies are another thing—take one movie that we use expressions from all the time, "The Wizard of Oz." "Over the rainbow," "down the yellow-brick road," "off to see the wizard," "the wicked witch of the west"—you've got stories full of these things. It can get really boring using a comma then a reference to the old Hollywood movie.

There's a joke that got into a story during the 1992 political campaign about George Bush, Dan Quayle, Ross Perot and Bill Clinton going to Oz, and how . . . Bush asks for a heart, Quayle asks for a brain, Perot asks for courage, Clinton wants to meet Dorothy. How does that translate in other nations? Not well, but can we cut that reference out of the taped versions of the story? If we do, do we change the story's essential meaning?

A teenager sneaks off from a prom to give birth in a bathroom— you have to ask yourself what's a "prom" to that reader in Peru? You have to explain it and just how bizarre it would be to go off and have something like that happen. We have one editor on the desk who's engaged to a Colombian woman, so he frequently calls her in the course of the day to submit these kinds of details. If she understands it, he'll put it on the wire in South America.

One of the advantages we do have is that the overseas audience has access to other sources of information for context on the United States. They may not be the most wonderful sources, or always the most objective and balanced sources—they're movies, TV shows, music, fashion. People around the world have a sense that they know the United States—or at least they do in Eastern Europe or China; they're getting to know the United States, and they're getting to know it fast. It takes a little bit of a burden off of us. We can sometimes assume that they've probably seen a movie that shows the New York subways, so if you report something happening in the New York subways, you can assume our audience may have a picture of it, or Central Park, or Hollywood or Texas.

I mention that because in a lot of the countries we do report from—a great majority of the countries that we report from—our reporters don't have that luxury. The news that goes out of a given country is about the only thing that at least Americans, and Germans and Chinese, too, are going to read about that society. For example, most of us are never going to visit Pakistan; maybe we'll see a movie from there, but how many people have seen a movie from Pakistan? How many people have read an author from Pakistan? So, the stories that the reporters send you from Karatsi are all you know about the country.

This is a complaint we get from Bosnians, from people who live in Belfast: that we're giving the world an incomplete picture. I won't argue that it's our responsibility to give them a complete picture, but I think we need to be, as journalists, sensitive to the fact that because of that distance, our information may be the only thing that people hear about a given culture. In cultures outside America much more is known about, for instance, pop culture.

John Belushi, not so very long ago, was still big news in Hong Kong. "Bay Watch" is watched in more countries than any other television show. I know, in my own experience, when I lived in Chile for three years, the prime-time show was "Get Smart." "Hogan's Heroes" is big in Germany now. With this exposure comes interest in celebrities behind these shows. They want to hear about them; they want to read about them. We'll give them the information. They want to read about sports. What's feeding that desire? Probably CNN, ESPN and others that now fill up time on cable networks. We get lots of demand for NFL now from Europe and from Mexico—places you wouldn't really think would embrace these sports.

Feeding this demand sometimes puts us in an awkward position. I wish I never had to print a story on a beauty pageant again. But, in many parts of the world, beauty pageants are huge stories—huge kinds of stories. We have to spend a lot of money covering them for the countries where our notion of political correctness doesn't coincide with that of local readers and viewers. In short, in some countries parading around in bathing suits for prizes is accepted.

Bill Gates may be the second most famous man around the world. Can anybody guess who's the first? Former Chicago Bulls forward and now NBA executive Michael Jordan. There's a huge market for stories about Jordan, just as there is for stories about Bill Gates and about technology and computers. One magazine in Brazil recently spent much of a monthly issue telling and showing its readers the layout of Gates' new house.

It's interesting to speculate about why this is exciting news for people. As I travel, I talk to foreign editors. Not too long ago I was speaking with an editor in Caracas, and it was amazing how closely his interests mirrored those of U.S. editors. He was looking for technology, health and medicine stories. Readers there say, give us more health and medicine stories. Give us animal stories; they like animal stories. They know the AP will always give them earthquakes and typhoons, and other tragedies. But they want these other stories, too, so we make a great effort to produce them.

Interestingly, these are the same interests that you hear from Americans—more health and medicine, technology, business, trade. It's interesting to think about why this is becoming a universal common interest among news media around the world. Corruption—stories about corruption—are playing big because there are stories about corruption in just about every country now. More and more sex scandals—even in countries where you couldn't believe that there would be a sex scandal.

I think readers and viewers are more interested in corruption and government reform because they're not so interested in ideology any longer. It doesn't really matter whether the government is communist or capitalist; almost all of them are capitalist these days. There's no interest in whether they're pro-U.S. or pro-Soviet, since the Soviet Union doesn't exist anymore. There's a lot less interest in what kind of government they have and more in how well the government is working.

The optimistic thing about this is that it may bring Americans back around to an increased interest in what's happening overseas. I think in a certain sense we're a little bit behind the curve of the rest of the world in having an ideological focus to our international news. It's the way we've always seen the "big picture," the world: in terms of us and them. Once we drop that focus, we may begin seeing the same shared interests that a lot of other countries are seeing.

In the news business, we're becoming more and more international all the time, in terms of where our reporters are and where they work. We recently sent an Australian to London; we sent a Briton to Argentina; we sent a Canadian to Jakarta. These people may bring different focuses to how we provide better coverage overseas. In the long run this may be part of a news "melting pot," one that, ideally, will bring Americans back around to reading and watching international news.

It won't mean that international journalism is going to get any easier. It will mean that perhaps we'll have to continue writing— going that extra step—to explain our stories, to provide the details, to write in a compelling fashion, to seize the opportunities to make a human story out of a very distant story, to avoid the cliche forms of journalism that we used for so very long, especially in our international reporting. That turned off a lot of readers.

We're going to have to avoid pack journalism, which, unfortunately, affects much of international journalism. It's a big problem. It's an insult to readers and viewers, who get the notion that journalists all agree on what the story will be, and different media release that same story and only one version of the story. I think readers and viewers are smarter than that. We'll have to continue to do all these things to make sure that distance is as safe as we can possibly make it. That's the challenge, and today's technology makes it both easier and harder.

We now have laptops that are smaller than my old-fashioned briefcase. We can sit down with them in the forests of Rwanda and file our stories to New York. All we have to do is take the top off, position it toward the satellite, push a button, and start to write. We can file photographs this way, too. Television still requires the suit-case-sized satellite phones, but they'll soon be really tiny, and we can use them anywhere. They're almost as useful for us in cutting down the distances around the world as the explosion of telephones. It wasn't too long ago when Zaire was having a revolution—now it's the Congo—and I needed to talk to our reporter there. I had her cell phone number and called her up. There was a problem with a story. She said, "Kevin, can I call you back in about 15 minutes?" Being the busy boss, I said, "Why?" She said, "I'm kind of crouched down in an alleyway here, and there's some shooting going on." I said, "Well, okay, call me back." I'm pretty sure she was telling the truth. I've used a few lies to get my editors off my back sometimes, too, but I think this one was telling the truth.

We have this ability to connect, instantly, with our reporters, and have our reporters connect instantly with us, that didn't exist 10 years ago. Back then they had satellite phones, too, but they were really bulky, and you needed a generator. There's no place on earth where we can't get to the story. We get to typhoons out in the middle of nowhere. I personally think that the massacre in Rwanda would have gone largely unreported 10 years ago, or 15 years ago, or certainly would not have been anywhere as near well covered if we hadn't had the technological means that we have now.

All the advances aren't technological. In a sense we can create our own army, and we have. We've gone to Somalia and hired our personal guards. We've gone to Bosnia and bought special, armour-plated Mercedes and flack-jackets that will cover you from your chin to your toes. We will travel around with armed guards, in armed cars, with our own means of communication. You saw us! You saw us when the Marines landed in Somalia. We were there! You saw us when they landed in Bosnia. They did it a lot more low-key, because they looked kind of ludicrous storming the beach while the journal-ists were there in shorts. So, when they got to Bosnia, they kept it a little more low-key, because they knew we were waiting there with our notebooks. But we were there. We've been in situations where they've called on us and said, "Hey, I need to call my headquarters; can I use your phone?"

So, we have this wonderful technology to get to the stories—to be there and cover our stories independently. I'll let you decide whether we're better off for it or not. I think readers are, but I'm not sure we are. It creates a problem for reporters because editors can call you up when you're crouching behind that wall and tell you to change your story. Editors have more power than reporters have with this new technology. Back when a reporter sent his dispatch and it took days to reach his editor, the editor tended to leave it alone a little bit more. Why? Because if he had a question, he might not be able to get back to the reporter anyway, so he had to trust in the reporter's judgment and expertise.

Technology brings us so close to the story—allows us to quote so many people—that we can forget what's a good quote and what's a bad quote, and simply provide people with too much information. We can provide them with useless information; we can provide them with useless color and useless quotes. Because of the technology, there's now no limit on the number of words we can transmit. There's no limit on the number of people we can interview. There's no limit on the number of stories we can move. We have to keep in mind that there is a limit on anybody's capacity—to read, to watch, to view—that's an easy limit to forget.

The desire for the "instant story" that lightning fast communications make possible creates an almost addiction to immediacy. People want news instantly, and if they don't get it, they move on. We can get caught up in providing updates, updates and more updates, and never reflect on what the story is really about. We can neglect the need for analysis and for depth. That's one of the biggest problems that we face. Our words, pictures and images reach far beyond our desktops and laptops. For those whose lives they touch in lands far from New York, Los Angeles or Peoria, they can create either balance or distortion.

CHAPTER 4

American News, Global Audience

János Horvát

Citizens of foreign countries are permanently uneasy about the U.S. media. The recurrent complaints are: "We are marginalized. Americans do not care about the rest of the world. They don't understand us." One might think these complaints have only to do with an inferiority complex inherent in smaller countries and that the Russian media—also that of a big nation—would provoke similar criticism. But they don't.

The American media are special because they have become international. American stories are read, watched and analyzed all over the world. As András Szántó and I observed in a monograph in 1993, U.S. journalism has gone global and can no longer cater to a public that is detached, geographically, politically and philosophically, from the rest of the world. Furthermore, the international audience that U.S. news organizations serve is comprised of many influential professionals and policy-makers who make decisions based on reports and information generated by those media organizations. And lastly, U.S. journalists inform a domestic public that elects public officials who influence world affairs.

Before the global transformation wrought by World War II, American journalism could afford to be isolated, to cater to a public

János (pronounced YOHN-osh) Horvát is media adviser to Centoro Film in his native Budapest, Hungary. He is also a former senior adviser to Magyar Televizio (Hungarian Television) and was a 1990 fellow of the Gannett Center. The essay that follows was originally published in *Media Studies Journal* (Fall 1995), which has granted permission for its reprint in this volume.

with relatively little interest in world affairs. Today such journalism is at odds with the powerful roles that America and American journalism play in the world at large. In foreign reporting the golden rule of the American media—the strict separation of facts and editorial opinion—can lead to misunderstandings. Readers and viewers need interpretive voices to guide them through a jungle of facts, especially when the facts are reported from a distant and unfamiliar part of the world. In foreign reporting, interpretive journalism would help American readers to better understand international affairs. A move away from "fact-based" reporting would not necessarily signify a move toward partisan bias. The West European press successfully integrates news and editorials. Its journalists present fact-based international news reports in which all sides of the story are faithfully included, yet are balanced by the reporters' own well-informed views that are based on firsthand experience in the region and a thorough understanding of the events.

To the lack of interpretation we can add the problem of discontinuity in reporting. One of the key structural problems of American media is the intermittent coverage of issues that might rest for a while but then become important overnight.

American editors, when faced with interesting news from a foreign country, immediately dispatch reporters to the scene. The machinery quickly goes into full swing, even in the most remote spot on the globe. However, when a given "revolutionary" period is over, the coverage stops abruptly, the scene is abandoned and years pass until the country is on the agenda again. Then American journalists, instead of following the original story, have to restart from scratch. Names, politicians maybe even borders have been changed without having been reported. No familiar facts or figures remain. This phenomenon exists in print journalism, but it is extremely manifest in television news. And it becomes ever more important when reporters have to move from the coverage of dramatic events to the coverage of complex issues.

The Romanian Revolution of 1989 is a good example of this phenomenon. It was quick, crammed with events, and the opposing groups were easy to tell apart—at least in the beginning. A genuine popular revolt against a cruel dictatorship broke out in mid-December 1989 in the city of Timisoara, close to the Hungarian border. Then, on Dec. 21, in Bucharest, during a hastily organized pro-Communist rally, one dissenting voice was enough to turn the crowds against the dictator Nicolae Ceausescu and his wife, Elena. Security forces tried to quell the insurgency, but the army joined in the uprising. The revolution's headquarters were in the building of the state-run TV, and the rapidly evolving events were transmitted live to Romanians and the world. By Christmas the hiding dictator was captured, brought to trial and executed. In one short week, one of the cruelest Communist dictatorships in history sank into oblivion.

Correspondents arriving by air flew straight into the chaotic fighting around the airfield and witnessed shooting, rolling tanks, capturing of security officers, and faced a great deal of uncertainty about just who the enemy was. After the execution, it was still possible to cling to the more comfortable genre of "event" reporting until "issues" started to gain over "events." And where "issues" must be handled, clichés start slipping in when there is no hard evidence, no certain sign about the future.

The narration of a short and simple event is relatively easy. Perhaps the advantage of TV reporting in an "emergency situation" is that the images convey so much that there is little need to add anything else, while the short time frame doesn't necessitate any incidental stories or unnecessary conjectures. Powerful images and limited time make for realistic and penetrating news. But when events turn murky and ideological and the revolutionary fervor disappears—as in Romania—TV news loses its firm footing. It is less able to cope with the growing number of opinions, sources and the increasing complexity of the situation. Rather than playing a key role, images become superfluous—and may even prevent important news from being conveyed. At this point, the big networks tend to drop the previously interesting item, which finds its way onto ABC's "Nightline," where it attracts about half the audience of ABC's "World News Tonight."

The amount of coverage given to Romania smoothly descended like the downward slope of a bell-shaped curve, revealing not only the decreasing importance of the whole event but also the limited capability of TV news to deal in depth with complex issues. It is somehow symbolic that the American networks turned melancholic in the last days of the year as they bid farewell to the cataclysm of the Romanian revolution, which had offered an excellent opportunity to brandish the best of American TV journalism. Since then, Romania has hardly popped up on American TV screens. In 1993, for example, Romania did not appear on a single weekday newscast on the three leading U.S. networks.

The problem is hardly unique to coverage of Eastern Europe. Not only Romania, but Haiti and Somalia—just to name a few— have also been lost behind the scenes. And this amnesia will probably determine the fate of Bosnia as well.

American television news is a narrative genre that attempts to provide a unified interpretation of all the events of a given day. American anchors act as narrators drawing possible links between the various items, a technique not customary in Europe. The narrative style is time-consuming. In January 1995, in the 22 minutes of the evening news programs, ABC, CBS and NBC had 15 news items as an average in their news programs. In Hungary, this number is 22–25. (A few years ago, that number was 25–30, but it has been decreasing sharply as the narrative style gains acceptance in Hungary also.)

Stories on television always tend to have an ending. Real life does not. In our example, with the death of the Romanian dictator the TV story was over, but the real story was just beginning to unfold. The new government was almost immediately voted out of power. Ethnic rivalries flared up. But the scene was already abandoned by the American press, to be revisited when the next dictator or monarch would be overthrown. Obviously there is justification for this interruption of coverage. Limited space on the pages and limited time on the screen leave little room for less sensational international politics. But that also reflects the fact that the United States feels less vulnerable to international events. In this view, America and its press can afford to be isolated.

The European press has always been more sensitive to the outside world. The British are traditionally "imperial" minded. A train collision in a remote province of Pakistan might be a story, because the British—being once at the center of a huge empire—still feel that any collision of a crowded train might be followed by unrest, where angry protesters, mourning their relatives, can turn their grief against the "oppressor" who operates the train despite poor and sometimes dangerous conditions. The accident can be a spark, igniting a chain of serious political troubles. The coverage will be continuous; reporters will return to the site, always keeping a sharp eye on the events.

But we can also mention the German or French press, where unimportant events in the Polish or Latvian parliament are reported on a regular basis. The different geopolitical ambiance gives a special importance to the news coming from countries that can directly influence the fate of another nation.

Journalism, in both domestic reporting and foreign coverage, is a translation process that converts distant, foreign and abstract notions into stories that make sense. Yet sometimes interesting phenomena are sacrificed for the sake of a story line, and the uniqueness of an event is lost forever.

On the first day of the Romanian upheaval, revolutionaries seized the building that housed the state-run TV—the only television network in the country—setting the stage for an unprecedented media event. For a few days the TV studio not only played host to the news but was also part of it. Instead of a structured, live transmission or news coverage, uncensored and unedited reality exploded onto the TV screen. There were no scripts, plans or control. In Romania, the image made history. It was a happening unlike any other seen in the history of television.

But the true importance of this remarkable incident in Romania has never been fully discovered by the American media. On American screens, the European tradition of storming newspaper offices, which goes back to the revolutions of 1848–1849, was stressed only by correspondents who recognized this special episode's roots in media history. Editors and anchors did not point out that the pictures coming from Romania were not news coverage, but the revolution itself. To explain the relevance of the event, they would have had to delve into a time-consuming explanation of the European TV system of how in Eastern Europe in 1989 there was only one kind of TV—state TV—and that to storm the TV building was to attack one of the most visible icons of one-party state rule. It was a direct affront to existing government. To explain all this would have required extra time, extra length. So this essential dimension was simply eliminated from the stories.

Correspondents attempting to make sense of such confusing events will often attempt to provide explanations in the form of sound bites from "ordinary people." But sound bites tend to support journalistic findings rather than to originate them. Street interviews usually function as a prologue to a story or as illustrations to emphasize the multifaceted reality. Listening to the voice of the people is a standard fixture in reporting on revolutions and upheavals, where popular support is always more important than the opinion of one or two politicians. These street interviews add color, feelings and passion to the rigid reality of any power struggle.

It is a rule of thumb for American TV journalists working in foreign countries to find English-speaking interviewees for the evening broadcast. This is easier today than it was 20 years ago. Foreign politicians, journalists and opposition people speak English in increasing numbers. But not all of the people on the streets of foreign capitals speak English. In certain cases, like earthquakes, locals will be dubbed by an interpreter whose accent sounds foreign. But the primary goal is to find as many English-speaking (or muttering) indigenous people as possible. (In contrast, non-English-language TV stations in Europe or Asia usually conduct interviews in the local vernacular.) In an American television broadcast, the messages carried by "foreign" sound bites are rather dubious. Together with tears and smiles, they express human emotions. But, more often than not, they also carry a secondary message. Many American viewers are probably impressed by Serbians speaking English, evoking the false impression that "over there" even bus drivers speak English. They are unaware of the tedious search of the TV journalist to spot someone who was able to put together a short sentence.

There are hidden and unconscious consequences to such coverage. Below the sweeping and dynamic pictures of the revolution, there is an ocean of poorly dressed and uneducated people who cannot properly express their thoughts and who can only mumble about freedom and democracy. Though American viewers in their multicultural society are familiar with fractured English, they would be unlikely to sympathize with the cause or issue at hand when faced with a muttering and mumbling populace. Unwittingly, encounters with foreigners speaking clumsy English also stir an air of superiority. Even if the camera is leveled at these faces, it appears as though we are looking down on them.

This distorted perspective is a consequence of the fact that the American press is a self-contained institution. Its readers, viewers and critics are basically Americans. It is always analyzed from American perspectives. Scrutinizing the American media from a distant and different viewpoint is always challenging. Foreign critics can be biased or one-sided, but from time to time a small country or seemingly unimportant event can serve as a good magnifying glass when experts want to focus on media issues that have always been examined by domestic standards.

The close-to-perfect technical possibilities of American broadcasting are not always matched with well-prepared journalists. In the typical, short evening news item, this ignorance might not be visible—but over the long term such coverage can lead to confusion. The appearance and disappearance of countries on television screens produce a special feeling of imbalance. Many times, instead of journalistic realism, the viewer gets a dispersed mosaic of events. The long, unedited mirroring of reality, and the dramatic episode of spot-news coverage, cannot substitute for thoroughness and understanding.

PART II

Global News and Cultural Values

CHAPTER 5

The Role of Cultural Values in Determining What Is News

Corey Flintoff

In many ways, those of us who watched, read or heard the media coverage of former President Bill Clinton's affair with an intern named Monica Lewinsky experienced a remarkable example of how media influences culture, culture influences media, and the technological changes in news and information and entertainment are driving these influences into a faster and faster cycle—a cyclone, almost.

Tired as we may have become of the Monica Lewinsky case back in 1998, it now serves to provide us with a framework for discussing how news media—American and international—are changing, and how those changes are influencing how news is covered and delivered. It is also a lesson in how media reflect, and at the same time influence American culture, and how cultural values affect the news. Reporting is a messy job, and publishing—or broadcasting—is a messy business. The operative words here are *job* and *business*. You

Corey Flintoff is best known as the news anchor of "All Things Considered" on National Public Radio (NPR). Throughout his career at NPR, he has covered stories ranging from abortion in Ireland to the Whitewater Hearings, from Congress to the White House, the State Department, and the Pentagon. A television documentary produced by Mr. Flintoff, "Eyes of the Spirit," is still being shown at the Museum of the American Indian in New York City. In 1989, he and his wife, Diana Derby, won a Corporation for Public Broadcasting Award for their coverage of the Exxon Valdez oil spill. He also teaches radio production and news writing at George Washington University, and is an occasional lecturer at John Hopkins University. The essay that follows is the edited transcript of a lecture given by Mr. Flintoff at the University of Rhode Island in 1998.

75

start getting in trouble when the business starts to interfere with the job, and people with jobs start to think that they're in business. To a degree, I think that's what stories like the one that captured the nation's—and world's—attention back in 1998 illustrate.

Let's go back, for a moment to 1998, and look at the news horizon before the Monica Lewinsky story. There were at least three important domestic stories on the news horizon: the federal budget, tobacco litigation and campaign fund raising. There were three potentially history-changing international stories on the horizon: the possibility of another war with Iraq, the Asian financial crisis and the bird flu in Hong Kong. We could add the El Nino weather phenomena. There was Pope John Paul II in Cuba, the possibility of the first steps toward renewal. But what happened?

On January 21, 1998, Monica Lewinsky changed inalterably what Americans considered—and consumed—as news. In the week just prior to the Lewinsky situation breaking through from the Internet to mainstream news media, the three major broadcast networks spent time on several big international news stories: an East Asian bank crisis led the pack, and the Iraq-UN arms inspections came next. Again, this is the week just before "zippergate." The following week, once the Lewinsky affair was in full throttle, news priorities changed dramatically. Clinton's sexual affair and possible perjury not only led every network newscast during the week of January 21, 1998, but, compared with the previous week, had three times the amount of exposure, in total minutes, as did Iraq.

During that week, Iraq, which had been the top story, was bumped down to the fourth most important story; the total time dedicated on all networks to the pope's Cuba visit was 42 minutes; for the Iraqi arms inspections total time spent was 11 minutes. The two taken together received a total of 53 minutes on all three networks versus 111 minutes devoted to Clinton's sexual affair. The Unabomber trial got only 10 minutes. Even the Asian financial crisis—and that's about people's money, a so-called pocketbook issue—received short shrift.

By the second week of the Clinton-Lewinsky sexual affair situation, things heated up even more for the intern and cooled down even more significantly for international coverage. We now received 1,300 minutes on the Clinton sexual affair on the three networks. Monica Lewinsky received 807 minutes, the Paula Jones sexual harassment case 790 minutes. By a 5:1 ratio the sex scandal story got more airtime than the Iraq-UN ban, and even the State of the Union address got a meager 24 minutes compared with 125 minutes devoted to the president's affair.

I'm not implying that the Monica Lewinsky story wasn't important then or that it has no historical significance. The potential fall of the American administration could have a lot of impact on other countries in the world, but let's face it. We as Americans have lived through disgrace of an American president before, and we've survived. We even survived the rehabilitation of Richard Nixon as an elder statesman.

So, it seems to me that the real danger here is that the American news media and the American public can be distracted from some of the very critical issues that face us at the outset of the 21st century. The real danger here is time wasted, time lost. When we see how many minutes were devoted, how much time we spent on this story—and it's just a microcosm of the kind of story that threatens to detract from coverage of international or global news of some significance—we see that the threat is that history will repeat itself more ferociously than we can possibly imagine.

What about the financial crisis in Asia? It got pushed off the radar screen of news organizations during the fever to reveal the next tidbit of information about the White House intern. What are the ramifications of losing sight of such a story? The worst-case scenario might be a domino effect, bringing nation after nation to its knees—a worldwide depression. Maybe four to 10 years of international financial distress. Maybe the rise of totalitarian regimes. I don't mean to belabor this point, but I grew up among people who lived through the Great Depression, and they never forgot what it did to them. They never forgot that there's a very thin veneer, a very thin illusion, of the control that people have over their own financial destiny. Those people are your great grandparents, or your grandparents, and in my case, my parents. They remember these things, and what we all tend to forget now is that these really big financial upheavals take a long time to play out.

We don't know what would happen if Asian countries didn't buy our greens and our soybeans and our rice, not just for one year, but for four years, or six years or 10 years in a row. Alan Greenspan doesn't know. The administration is afraid, and rightly so, that a flood of cheap exports from these Asian countries that are in such financial distress will round out American exports all over the world. Remember that the Great Depression lasted from 1929 until its effects became too muddled to measure by the effects of World War II. We tend to underestimate the winding effect, the long-term loss of markets we have. The problem is we just don't know, and we'll *never* know if news organizations forsake coverage of stories with global significance in favor of fleeting glimpses of 21-year-old former interns.

Just to complete my grim, little triangle, consider the bird flu in Hong Kong. It seems like it was a pretty small thing, but at the time, you may recall, it was a very big story, a very important story. Health authorities seemed to have acted remarkably quickly and decisively to bring it to an end. It even seemed a bit ridiculous when there was this slaughter of millions of chickens in Hong Kong; it seemed like nothing became of it. Maybe it worked! We don't know that. We do know that plagues periodically wipe out large numbers of our species.

The Spanish flu in 1918–1919 wiped out something like 20 million people in a little under two years, killing two million people in the United States alone in under seven months. It's true that we have much better medical response methods today, but it's also true that we have a much larger total population. We have transportation that would allow the next plague to strike simultaneously all over the globe. Actually, health experts anticipate that there's going to be another plague. It may not be the bird flu, but it could be something similar.

With all this on the horizon, the fate of Bill Clinton and his Oval Office lover would seem to be just a little bit less compelling. Even so, why Monica? Why this story? There are certain changes in modern media culture that allow such scandal to displace important news. For one thing, news is assembled quicker today; because of the rise in Internet news, netcasting, a factoid or a rumor can be out there for public consumption in the time it takes to log on and to type. Because of the advent of the 24-hour news channels—CNN, MSNBC, the Fox News Channel—people can turn on news like their water faucet now. It's becoming a utility like electricity.

Second, there's a glut of media all the way from the Internet to the *New York Times.* And the Lewinsky story, as we'll see, appeals to all of them. As Howard Kurtz wrote in the *Washington Post,* "It has both a titillation factor and the political gravity to span the entire media."

Finally, I think the level of public discourse in the United States has become much coarser than it used to be. It's no longer taboo to discuss the sex life of the president; it's no longer taboo to discuss oral sex, or semen stains, on the nightly news. I think there are a lot of factors to blame for the loss of restraint in public discourse.

First and foremost, I blame my own generation for thinking that free speech meant guilty speech, for thinking that everything that we thought needed to be said. I'm appalled now at how childish and self-centered we were. Second, I blame the entertainment media, which are now solidly in the hands of my generation, for trying to find out just how vulgar the next situation comedy or the next movie can be.

I'm heartened by the fact that many people all the way from the junior high school generation right through to my own generation, seem to be getting tired of this. But I'm disheartened by the fact that neither the entertainment media nor the news media seem to be aware of that fact. These three things—information speed, increased media outlets and the level of public discourse—set the stage for the Lewinsky story and the way that it would be played.

Remember, too, that when the Lewinsky story appeared, the last big tabloid story was the death of Princess Diana; by the advent of the presidential intern scandal that story had substantially faded, despite the efforts of all the talk shows and tabloids to keep it alive. We had full-tilt Diana retrospectives, you'll remember, 30, 60 and even 90 days after her death. Even that wasn't enough to keep the talking heads talking. The talk shows and the tabloids needed more; they needed these personality stories to keep them going.

They mostly managed to eat their way along with things like the British nanny case, the Jon Benet Ramsey case and Marv Albert. Nothing had rescued the talk shows and the tabloids like the death of Princess Diana. But, with the princess's death fading in memory, there was a vacuum of the kind of news—fast, cheap news—that could be covered by, for instance, staking out somebody's apartment house. In the Lewinsky story, once again, the 24-hour news networks and the talk shows had a perfect subject, easy to photograph and even easier to understand, since who doesn't understand or, at least say they understand, the basic precepts of sex?

You'll recall, by the way, what the initial problem was with the Monica Lewinsky case. You can graph the progress of the Lewinsky case by the timing of when the pictures became available. First, you'll recall, there was nothing but that big yearbook picture of Monica with the big hair. Then, later on, there was a picture of her in the low-cut dress with the gifts in front of her. For some reason, that picture with the low-cut dress appeared every time mention was made of the fact that the president may or may not have given her a dress, and whether she had possessed a dress that had DNA evidence of her relationship with the president. So, regardless of what the talking heads happened to be talking about when that particular image was on the screen, I don't see how any viewer could possibly have avoided the connection that this must have been the dress that he gave Monica Lewinsky.

When the Monica story broke, all three networks had their big anchors out in Havana, as you recall, covering the pope's visit to Cuba. Suddenly, they dropped the pontiff like a cold potato, and hot-footed it home. For six days, Monica stories clogged the airways. I think most viewers were just too stunned to react! But by the sixth day, the backlash began. People complained that they were sick of the coverage and sick of the way the media was swarming all over it.

By the second week of February in 1998, 56 percent of the people who responded to a *Washington Post* poll said they thought the media were treating President Clinton unfairly. Nearly three-fourths of the people in that poll, and also in the poll that was conducted by CNN at the same time, said they thought the Lewinsky story was getting too much coverage. The Freedom Forum did a poll, and in it it said the media are mostly interested in attracting a large audience. But despite all the complaints, a large audience is exactly what the media were getting. During the peak two weeks of the Lewinsky coverage, CNN and MSNBC doubled their ratings. Fox News Channel ratings went up by 121 percent in the first week. *USA Today* distributed 500,000 extra copies of its newspaper in a single day. Newsstand copies of *Time* magazine were increased by an extra 100,000 copies.

Not everyone rushed to print or to broadcast. A very good reporter by the name of Michael Isokoff works for *Newsweek,* and had covered the Whitewater investigation since it began. I first met Michael when NPR was broadcasting the Senate Whitewater Hearings, and we used him as a commentator. I have a lot of respect for the care he gave to the coverage of the Lewinsky story. Very early on, Isokoff had the story for *Newsweek,* but the magazine, after a lot of painful consideration, decided it wasn't ready to go with it.

So, along came Matt Drudge, who got wind of this story, and put it on his Internet "Drudge Report" on January 17, 1998. By the next morning, it was being discussed on ABC's "This Week," then on an NBC talk show, then on CBS radio. *Newsweek* was in a fix, because it had already passed its publication time, and it hadn't gone with the story. In the earlier days of news, a weekly magazine that passed on a story would have to wait seven days before getting another chance. The delay gave time for reflection.

When *Newsweek* saw that Isokoff's story was slipping away from it, *Newsweek* immediately put it on its *Newsweek* Web site. Even this didn't prove fast enough. On Wednesday, January 21, it broke onto the network news and the major newspapers. In news coverage today, we spend an awful lot of time watching what the other media are doing. The effect becomes one of following the leader, not becoming the leader. And the good news is that the public does appear to notice, at least eventually.

By mid-February 1998, when the news media began doing stories on the news media coverage of this story, people started telling reporters that not only did they not want to know more about the allegations, they felt that the coverage had been too graphic, especially the discussions about oral sex and semen-stained dresses on national television. In a *Washington Post* article around that time, people complained about x-rated news and said they didn't want their children listening to the news at dinnertime.

At NPR we had an ongoing newsroom debate about just exactly how to characterize this alleged relationship, and we wound up deciding to call it just an "alleged sexual relationship" without specifying just what sort of relationship it may have been. Our managing editor, Bruce Drake, insisted that we have a higher standard of confirmation for all the information that we use. That was a good thing, because it helped us avoid some of the same problems experienced by *The Wall Street Journal* and *The Dallas Morning News,* both of which had to retract lead stories they used when their sources went bad on them.

The major network news anchors disagreed on how the story should have been handled. Dan Rather, from CBS, said that he disliked it; he didn't get into news reporting to follow sex scandals, he said. He added that he thought the story was no good for the country and that nobody would come out of it looking good. At ABC, though, Peter Jennings likened the Lewinsky scandal to people rubbernecking at a car wreck. He said that even though this may not be the media's finest hour, at the same time he didn't think that the media had done anything wrong in the way they were covering the story. He called it a "political, social, and ethical story."

Actually, the media was tougher on the media than the public. A Committee of Concerned Journalists published a story showing that the coverage of the Lewinsky case had routinely mixed opinion and speculation. Forty-one percent of reporting on the Lewinsky case was either analysis, opinion or speculation: "The picture that emerges is of a media culture that is increasingly involved with assembling information, rather than gathering." Tom Rosensthal, who's a media critic and vice chairman of the Committee of Concerned Journalists, said that there was very little effort on the part of the media to say, "This source that we are talking about may have an ax to grind, and this is what the ax may be."

The report also criticized a lot of the language that was used by the media, particularly those reports that used the term *scandal,* and I tend to agree with that. I think it's too judgmental. I don't think it's a scandal until it has actually been proven to have happened; early on, the term was used carelessly. But, on the other hand, Carl Bernstein, the reporter who broke the Watergate story, laughed at that. He said, "If it looks like a duck, walks like a duck, and all the rest of it—this is a duck!"

Nevertheless, the speed that we command as journalists demands that we be that much more careful. Given that the public says it doesn't like stories like the Lewinsky affair, and much of the media seem to be a little bit ashamed of such stories, does that mean that they'll eventually disappear from news coverage? I doubt it. The public doesn't dislike scandal enough, whether they say they do or not. Remember that it took six days of absolutely relentless and mind-numbing coverage before people started to complain about it. We in the news media don't dislike it either, because storytelling is what we do. No matter what stories it replaced or what stories it eclipsed, for a time, in 1998, the Lewinsky story was, for all the issues of taste and judgment it raises, a good story.

If you go back and look at newspapers from around the turn of the century, and I mean newspapers that are now highly respectable organs, you'll find that in their early days they were virtually tabloids, too. They were packed with photos; they loved to use artists' depictions of crimes, and similar techniques. They published renderings of crimes, wars and goldrushes, and, yes, sex scandals. Besides, if you look at the biggest stories that are grist for this kind of coverage, you'll see that they're not far removed from folktales, or fairytales.

You have the hero who kills his wife in a jealous rage; that's right out of the great Greek tragedies. If you make it a black hero who kills his white wife, it's right out of Shakespeare. You have the fairytale princess who marries the not-so-fairytale prince, and finally finds love with somebody else. You have the story of the young girl who goes to the palace of the powerful king and then he either saves her life or she gets a share of his kingdom. So, we've been telling these stories for thousands of years, and I don't think we're going to stop any time soon.

The best thing we can do as reporters-storytellers, is to be *aware* of what we're doing. We have to be aware of the demands of this new technology and not be ruled by it or rushed by it into making judgments that we shouldn't make. We need to be aware of the types of stories that interest us and other human beings, and not be seduced by them. Most of all, we need to remind ourselves that the advent of technology opens up opportunities for more news coverage, not less—so that the choice need not be one made between stories about sex and stories about government or the economy. The choice need not be made between stories that occur within our borders and those in lands so far away that we may not immediately recognize their names, let alone their politics. There's room for both and for much more.

CHAPTER 6

News Through Alien Filters: The Impact of Imported News on a Small Nation

Paul Norris

Introduction

Some countries find the lure of cheap, proven, U.S. programming irresistible. One such willing U.S. satellite is New Zealand, where most of the programs on the channels watched by the young are from the United States. But when it comes to news, how far the American influence pervades is more complex.

Because the media in New Zealand cannot afford to maintain their own foreign correspondents, they have adopted a scavenger approach, acquiring news from wherever they can. The result is a diverse mix of international agencies and sources, and if there is a prevailing cultural influence it is not American but British. When one remembers that earlier generations of New Zealanders thought of Britain as "home," this may be seen as an enduring hangover from the days of the British Empire. Or it could simply be journalistic

Paul Norris has spent almost 30 years in television journalism, first working for the BBC in London as an expatriate New Zealander, then returning as director of news and current affairs for TVNZ from 1987 to 1994. He was a senior executive with TVNZ until 1996, when he took up the position of head of the New Zealand Broadcasting School at Christchurch Polytechnic.

conservatism. Whatever the reason, the pattern is at its most evident in television news, where the style may be American but where the overwhelming majority of imported reports are from the BBC or Britain's ITN, rather than CNN or the U.S. networks.

The New Zealand Environment

New Zealand is a small, thinly populated and remote country. Its population, at 3.6 million, is comparable with that of Ireland or the state of Colorado. Its nearest neighbor, Australia, is a three-hour flight away. But characteristics mitigate against physical isolation—many people read and travel widely, and new technology is eagerly embraced. Use of the Internet is among the highest in the world, at 35 percent of the population.

However, there is no national newspaper. Each of the four main urban centers has a morning newspaper that also circulates widely in the associated rural areas. Although there are a considerable number of provincial and community newspapers, international news is provided only by the four "metropolitan" dailies; an evening newspaper in the country's capital city, Wellington; and two Sunday newspapers that distribute to most of New Zealand.

For most of the population, awareness of international news is derived from television. The two main television networks, TVNZ and TV3, each run an hour-long news program at 6 p.m., and compete strongly for stories and audience. Television news has always rated highly in New Zealand, and continues to do so, despite some fragmentation of audiences and the emergence of other attractions such as the Internet. TVNZ's news, "One News," consistently rates about 20 percent, whereas TV3's news, "3 News," rates about 8 percent.[1] "One News" is frequently the top-rating program for the week and is always in the top three.

Television has been deregulated since 1988. This effectively means that TVNZ is the only state-owned broadcaster in the world to operate in a fully commercial manner, not subject to a charter or a legislated programming remit.[2] Formerly enjoying a monopoly of advertising revenue, since 1989, it has been obliged to compete with privately owned TV3. Critics have noted changes in the content and style of TVNZ's news presentation since deregulation, changes that are perceived as a "dumbing down" and a trend to more sensationalized or tabloid reporting. Some have attributed these developments to American influences, particularly TVNZ's use of American news consultants.[3]

Certainly the United States is the dominant cultural influence in terms of television entertainment programs and movies. Largely because it is a very small market that happens to speak English, New Zealand has one of the lowest levels of home-produced programming (known as local content) in the world. Across all programs on the three main channels, the level of local content is 23 percent.[4] The balance is imported, mostly from the United States, with other programs coming from Britain and Australia. For TV2 (target audience 18–39) and TV3 (target audience 18–39), the overwhelming proportion of programs is American—the most popular including "The Simpsons," "Friends," "Ally McBeal," "ER," "Chicago Hope," "The Practice," "Sex and the City" and "The Sopranos." A sample survey in 1998 found that more than 65 percent of the prime-time programming on these two channels was from the United States.[5]

There is also the question of media ownership. An extraordinary feature of deregulation was the decision, made by the government in 1990, to allow 100 percent foreign ownership of any media company. The privately owned television company TV3 is majority owned by CanWest, a global operator with stations in Canada, Australia and Ireland. The leading newspaper company INL, which publishes the two Wellington newspapers, another of the metropolitan dailies and a Sunday newspaper, is 49 percent owned by Rupert Murdoch's News Corporation.

INL is also the majority owner of Sky Television, the dominant pay TV operator. The largest commercial radio network, TRN, is owned by Tony O'Reilly's Independent News, Ltd., together with U.S. radio operator Clear Channel Communications, which has management rights and has made one of their people TRN's chief executive. TRN, in turn, owns the only commercial radio news organization, Independent Radio News (IRN).

It may be thought remarkable that a small nation that professes itself concerned to promote its own identity and culture should allow global operators to own and control all its private media organizations. Such global operators are primarily concerned with profits and efficiencies rather than the local culture. Regarding news, they prefer to import cheap material from global sources rather than invest in resources to ensure a New Zealand perspective.

The Effect of an Alien Filter

It may be helpful to distinguish the ways in which the dissemination of news may become subject to alien filters. At its most direct, this will take the form of a republication of material from a source outside one's own organization. This material may be intended for international distribution, such as that from a news agency, or it may be primarily intended for a domestic market, such as television news reports from the American networks, or newspaper columns syndicated in the United States.

Less directly, the news agenda of a small country may be influenced by the decisions seen to be taken by larger and more powerful news organizations, some of which portray themselves as having an international focus, for example, Reuters or CNN or BBC World. If they determine that the bombing of Kosovo, or the papal visit to the Holy Land, or President Clinton's relationship with that intern merits a certain level of coverage, then this must be a consideration for those creating a news program in Auckland. Who ultimately determines news values? Although this absorbing question cannot be answered here, it is enough to suggest that the stance taken by leading organizations does feed through to those farther down the food chain.

Then there may be issues of style and presentation in which the format and promotion strategies of a successful operator in a large competitive market may inspire imitation in a smaller market, particularly one that is moving into a more competitive phase. If it works for NBC or KCAL in Los Angeles, or the *Los Angeles Times* or the BBC, should we not follow the trend in New Zealand?

Television News and Current Affairs

Coverage of international events came of age with the use of satellites in the early 1980s. This enabled complete bulletins from major international broadcasters to be recorded in real time and selected reports extracted and replayed in New Zealand programs. Previously cans of overseas news film would be flown in to one center, be shown there and then flown on to the next city for further showing. By the time the films reached the southernmost center, stories could be weeks old.

Then came CNN. In 1990, Sky launched New Zealand's first pay TV service, with CNN one of the basic channels. By 1994, CNN had competition from BBC World, and TVNZ had access to both.

By this time the television news departments of both major networks had become accustomed to using a variety of sources of international news. Living off the international agencies and overseas networks is the only way they can hope to cover the world. This can be seen as a strength, as, for example, in the Persian Gulf War, when the two New Zealand networks used large numbers of reports from both British and American news organizations.

Live feeds became routine. Viewers could watch the daily media briefings live from the Pentagon, complete with official video footage of the smart bombs finding their targets. They witnessed the CBS reporter setting up his satellite dish in Kuwait City and his live reports as Allied troops recaptured the territory.

But they were also exposed to a range of different voices, from the likes of the BBC's Kate Adie or John Simpson. This plurality of sources provided viewers with an overall picture that was arguably more balanced than that received in either the United States or Great Britain, where news organizations relied primarily on stories from their own reporters. The scavenger enjoys the best of what can be gleaned from around the world.

To that end, both television news organizations have contracts with a wide variety of suppliers. TVNZ has contracts with CNN, CBS, Reuters, the BBC and Australia's Channel 9. TV3 has access to NBC, ABC, APTN, ITN and Australia's Channel 7.

The New Zealand networks have no difficulty in reusing reports lifted directly from American or British bulletins as received by satellite, complete with their original American or British voice tracks and reporter stand-ups. Their source is openly credited in the anchor throws—for example: "this report from CBS," or "the BBC's Jeremy Bowen reports." Whereas this would be unthinkable in major international news organizations, it seems entirely natural in a small country that wishes to maintain a high-quality international coverage.

The harsh economic reality is that, for the most part, news organizations in New Zealand are not prepared to commit to the cost of maintaining foreign correspondents. The chief exception is the state broadcaster TVNZ, which established its own reporters in London and Sydney in 1988. The rationale for such correspondents is that they provide stories of interest to New Zealand viewers that would simply not be covered otherwise, and that they deliver a New Zealand angle to some stories on the international agenda, an angle that would be missing otherwise. TVNZ has three foreign correspondents, one in London and two in Sydney, whereas TV3 has one, in Sydney.

The success of these correspondents underlines the special dimension they bring to New Zealand's international coverage and the void left in the absence of such coverage. Having a New Zealand journalist report from Berlin as the Wall comes down provides an immeasurable benefit over access to any other international source. Similarly, there can be nothing to match our man in Bosnia taking a sheaf of viewers' letters to Sarajevo to deliver personally to Melisa, a teenage victim of the conflict who first touched the hearts of New Zealand viewers with her tears and hopelessness in a satellite interview on the daily current affairs program "Holmes."[6]

Regrettably, these correspondents are the exception. For the most part, TVNZ and TV3 rely heavily on the use of reporters from overseas networks for their coverage of international stories. It is not unusual for several such stories to be carried in an hour-long bulletin, and sometimes it may be as many as four or five.

To illustrate this point, "One News" (TVNZ) carried the following reports within the bulletin of 25 March 2000:

Uganda mass suicide	Kathy Jenkins	BBC
Papal visit to Holy Land	Allen Pizzey	CBS
Anniversary of Kosovo		
bombing	Ben Brown	BBC
Chechnya: plight of		
Grozny	James Rogers	BBC
Oscars: preview	Tom Brook	BBC

This may be news through an alien filter, but it is certainly not an American one. In recent years, the popular "One News" has shown a marked preference for using BBC reports over those from its American sources. This is even true for essentially American stories. In the preceding example, the Oscars were previewed by a British reporter. Similarly, for President Clinton's visit to Pakistan in March 2000, "One News" used a report from the BBC's Mike Wooldridge. Reports on NASA's future plans and on the progress of the Microsoft antitrust case were both sourced to the BBC rather than an American view.

American reports were certainly available on these stories, from CNN or CBS, and American reports are used in some instances. However, in many cases producers prefer the BBC version, or for TV3 that from ITN. To what extent this is a matter of style, and to what extent there are sound journalistic reasons for this preference, cannot easily be determined. But this preference does lead to an interesting counterpoint with the cultural influences in imported programming, which tends to be overwhelmingly American, especially for the younger population.

Current Affairs' (news magazine) programs do not follow the news pattern, but tend to exhibit a marked American influence. TVNZ runs its version of "60 Minutes," and TV3 runs "20/20." Each of these programs runs some stories from the American parent, together with one or more local stories. Barbara Walters and Morley Safer are familiar faces. Recently, TV3 also has begun screening NBC's "Dateline," introduced by a local presenter.

But there are limits to the tolerance of the more extreme American reporting. In the early 1990s, TVNZ ran "Hard Copy" and "Inside Edition," but neither survived, even though "Inside Edition" was scheduled on TV2, the very American channel for younger viewers. Perhaps the tone was simply too tabloid and too alien.

American presentation style has certainly influenced news programs in New Zealand. TVNZ has used American news consultants since the early 1990s. Through their oversight, stories became tighter and sound bites shorter. Anchors interacted and showed themselves to be warm and human. The weather became more of a production. Bumpers, stings and teases were introduced to woo viewers back after commercial breaks.

Despite some opposition from the newsroom, reporters were persuaded to do more and more "live crosses,"—live intros to a story from the scene—and to be interviewed live from the studio. Gradually, the newsroom adapted to these requirements, and the reporters and anchors became more skilled at these tasks.

Decisions on these changes were made by TVNZ news management, who always retained editorial control, but the American consultants facilitated many of the developments. Furthermore, they believed strongly in the promotion of news, providing useful guidance to TVNZ's promotions department.

By the mid-1990s, TVNZ was producing an attractive and populist news bulletin, slick and accessible, fast-paced but with varieties of tempo. It was likened by some to the best in the local markets in the United States, for example, Los Angeles. Given the keen competition in such markets and the leading-edge approach adopted by some of the broadcasters, this may not have been an inappropriate comparison, although TVNZ was always concerned about producing national bulletins. Its competitor TV3 was following a similar philosophy and operating under similar international influences fostered by the channel's early alliance with NBC and its later ownership by CanWest.

Radio News

New Zealand offers plenty of choices in the radio market: There are almost 200 radio stations for its 3.6 million people. Most of these stations are commercial and take short news bulletins from the commercial news provider IRN, owned by The Radio Network, which also owns the largest number of stations.

Most of IRN's bulletins are of the headline variety, containing a limited number of audio tracks (stories voiced by a reporter). IRN subscribes to the international agencies AAP and Reuters for copy, but its primary supplier for reporter stories is CNN. On a major breaking story, it is likely that any first-hand report will be from CNN, but most days there will be few if any foreign tracks.

However, there is also a network of commercial news-talk stations, which provide a fuller news service and much discussion of topical issues. The news-talk network maintains a number of international stringers or freelancers who are not only used for comment on major stories but who also have a regular slot at least once a week. These stringers are based in America, Europe, Australia and Hong Kong, and it would be hard to conclude that any particular influence is predominant.

Having global owners does make a difference. The news-talk stations are run by The Radio Network, which is partly owned by Clear Channel Communications. On a running story in the United States, such as the custody battle over the Cuban boy Elian Gonzales, the news-talk network can access its sister stations owned by Clear Channel. This story achieved considerable prominence in New Zealand, and may be seen as an example of the potent influence of the news agenda flowing from the United States.

A comprehensive radio news service is offered by the public noncommercial channel National Radio, operated by the state-owned Radio New Zealand. Its approach is similar to that of BBC Radio 4, or National Public Radio in the United States. In addition to its hourly bulletins, it runs two extended news and current affairs programs daily: "Morning Report," from 6 to 9 a.m. and "Checkpoint," from 5 to 6 p.m. These programs invariably call on the expertise of a variety of reporters and correspondents worldwide. Although National Radio has a contract with CNN, whose reporters are used on occasion, most sources are likely to be non-American.

For most of its history, Radio New Zealand has employed a small number of foreign correspondents of its own. But in 1999, in response to financial pressures, this policy was abandoned in favor of a contract with the agency Feature Story News. This Washington, D.C.–based independent agency, founded by two British journalists in 1992, may be a harbinger of developments in international reporting. From its network of bureaus, correspondents and stringers, it claims to offer "customized" broadcast news to international broadcasters.

National Radio also runs a daily program called "Worldwatch." It contains feature reports on international stories, whose source is overwhelmingly British, mostly from the BBC, with additional material from Deutsche Welle and CNN. For followers of international issues, this program provides the most comprehensive and in-depth background and context of any media in New Zealand.

Much to the consternation of its commercial rivals, National Radio rates strongly in the major markets, particularly the capital city, Wellington. Through its "Morning Report," it can rightly claim to have some influence on politicians and opinion formers. It is therefore significant that National Radio does not offer a markedly Americanized version of events.

Newspapers and Magazines

The main New Zealand newspapers are the four metropolitan dailies, based in the four main cities and serving those cities and the surrounding areas. Each of these newspapers has a distinctly local or regional focus. There is no national daily newspaper. The closest approximations would be weekly publications, such as the two Sunday newspapers or the two weekly business newspapers. These four weeklies aim for nationwide distribution.

Because the main dailies have a local focus, it is unusual for international events to feature on the front page. Indeed, two of the dailies have a separate section devoted to "The World," where readers can expect to find the international news stories. Exceptionally important stories, or those with a local dimension, may be carried on the front page, with further material in "The World."

All such stories are sourced from international agencies, because no newspaper in New Zealand has its own foreign correspondents. The most frequently used agencies are Reuters and Associated Press (AP), with some newspapers also subscribing to Australian Associated Press (AAP) and Agence France Presse (AFP). On a random sample of the two dailies that publish a "World" section, the preferred source is clearly Reuters.

The core agencies are supplemented by access to several international newspapers for feature material. These include British sources such as *The Times,* the *Daily Telegraph, The Independent,* the

Guardian/Observer or *The Economist,* along with U.S. sources such as the *Washington Post* or the *Los Angeles Times.* Backgrounders on international issues are regularly found reprinted from these feature sources.

Newspaper editors enjoy considerable luxury of choice. *The Press,* the daily paper for the city of Christchurch, has a regular feature of international editorial comment, reprinting from at least 10 sources, including the *Financial Times,* the *Melbourne Age,* the *Boston Globe* and *The Wall Street Journal.* In the weekly *Sunday-Star Times,* international stories may be sourced to Reuters, AP, AFP, AAP, the *LA Times,* the *Gannett News Service* or the *Baltimore Sun.* In other sections of the newspaper, features may be found from *USA Today,* the *LA Times,* the *Sunday Times* (London) or *Planet Syndications.*

Given the diverse nature of these sources, it cannot be said that there is marked American influence pervading news or feature coverage in the newspapers. One newspaper editor believes the opposite is the case. His newspaper, for example, prefers to cover U.S. politics using material reprinted from British newspapers such as *The Times* or the *Daily Telegraph* because they "interpret" the scene in the United States. There is considerable force to this argument, which is similar to the television networks exercising a preference for using American reports on events in Northern Ireland, where British reporting may be through a rather narrow lens, or may simply assume too much understanding for a wider audience.

Two markedly American forces of influence are *Time* and *Newsweek* magazines. *Time* is published in a specific New Zealand edition, and *Newsweek* is reprinted in *The Bulletin,* published by ACP in Australia.[7] Both magazines occasionally run stories from New Zealand, which does provide an opportunity for readers to test the filters through which their coverage is being received. One such cover story concerned New Zealand retaining the America's Cup in 2000, which included the line that New Zealand had "snatched" the Cup from the United States in 1995. Readers may have wondered whether "snatched" was the right word to describe the famous 5–0 victory in San Diego.[8]

The Internet

With the rapid development of the Internet in recent years, a vast array of new international sources has become available, to citizens and broadcasters alike the world over. Any keen student or follower of a particular story can surf a number of Web sites, which are growing in number and in the complexity of what can be accessed, with streaming video increasingly common. New Zealand has a relatively high number of Internet users, at 35 percent of the population, but how they are using the Net is less clear—we do not have adequate figures for the use of news sites.

Whatever the attraction of the Net, there is little present indication that broadcast audiences are drifting away. Average peak-time audiences may be declining but the trend is very slow—only a point or two during the last decade.[9] It seems reasonable to assume that consuming news in the traditional passive way and exploring the Internet for one's news will continue to be complementary activities for some time to come.

For media in New Zealand, the Internet offers a rich new menu of sources from which to scavenge. Does a news organization really need foreign correspondents when it can access all this information directly from a reporter's desktop in Auckland? It is certainly true that the Internet is being mined as a resource by some reporters and news editors in New Zealand. They can find stories, they can research context and background, they can canvass reaction and they can even find sound bites and actuality. But this is not the same as providing a particular perspective on events in a particular country; in other words, the Net is another tool in the reporter's armory, but it cannot be a substitute for informed news and comment from a media organization's own correspondent.

Conclusion

New Zealand presents an environment where the media accept that they cannot offer a full range of news, information and comment from around the world from their own resources. Their response to this predicament is to create their own model of global news—a mosaic of rich variety culled from a multitude of imported sources, with the newspapers and airwaves brimming with a chorus of talents, a cacophony of foreign accents.

It may be argued that the public are well served by this diversity. Need we really be concerned that the perspective is seldom New Zealand's own, that we are receiving an interpretation of world events through a series of alien filters? To this it must be said that there will always be a distinct gap between the quality of story offered by one's own correspondents, crafted to resonate with the New Zealand public, and agency or stringer material, which is less finely targeted. Furthermore, we can have little control over the quality or focus of such imports; we must place our trust in Reuters or Feature Story News and have faith in the editors who make the selection for us.

Television is arguably the medium with the most impact, and there the environment is at its least stable. In recent years, politicians have floated the prospect of selling off the state-owned broadcaster, TVNZ. Given that there are no restrictions on foreign ownership, such a sale would have been likely to attract the interest of global operators such as Rupert Murdoch, or Australia's Kerry Packer. In those circumstances, all programming, including news and current affairs, would have been arranged through global deals and driven by the need to maximize global efficiencies and profits. The local dimension would undoubtedly have suffered.

As it happens, the last election, in November 1999, put into government a center-left coalition who are committed not only to retain TVNZ in public ownership, but also to give it a renewed public service mandate. There is to be a new imperative to foster national identity and culture, partly through a quota system to ensure certain levels of local programming across a range of genres. The prime minister has herself taken the portfolio of minister of culture.

While there can be no such quota system for news reports, such a change in the political climate cannot but reverberate through all media. It should fortify those who defend and justify the role of our few foreign correspondents. It may even encourage more of them, as a small nation peers through its alien filters and struggles to maintain a balance between taking advantage of global opportunities and nurturing that local perspective so vital to its people.

Notes

1. These ratings figures are the percentage of the 5+ audience. Ratings are PUTs, measured by peoplemeters installed in a representative sample of homes. Source: AC Nielsen.
2. TVNZ runs two channels: TV One, broadly for older information seekers, and TV2, for younger entertainment seekers.
3. See Joe Atkinson, "Hey Martha! The Reconstruction of One Network News," *Metro,* April 1994.
4. "1999 Local Content Survey, New Zealand on Air," Wellington, April 2000.
5. Paul Norris, "American Responsibilities in the Global Arena: Cultures Under Threat Speak Out" (paper presented at the BEA, Las Vegas, April 1998).
6. For the outstanding contribution of two of TVNZ's correspondents, see Liam Jeory and Cameron Bennett, *Foreign Correspondents* (Auckland: Hodder Moa Beckett, 1995).
7. *Time's* readership, at 246,000, compares with 896,000 for New Zealand's most widely read magazine, *New Zealand Women's Weekly.* Source: AC Nielsen.
8. "It's Double Magic: New Zealand Sails into History," *Time,* 13 March 2000.
9. Source: Media Trends March 2000, AC Nielsen.

CHAPTER 7

Visual Information in Egyptian Television News: A Cross-cultural Influence

Hussein Amin

Egyptian Televison News: Function and Structure

Television news in Egypt is the primary source of news and information for most Egyptians. The main charge of televised news media in Egypt is to convey news and information of general interest, comment on events as well as provide opinion and perspectives. The purpose is also to reinforce social norms and cultural awareness through the dissemination of information about the culture and the society, to provide specialized data for commercial promotion and services and, finally, to entertain.[1] Egypt's theater tradition and long-established film and radio industry have provided the talent for television news that has not only enabled Egypt to generate and produce most of its own television news stories, but also has provided television news products to the Arab world.[2]

A member of the Egyptian Ministry of Information, Hussein Amin teaches in the department of journalism and mass communication at the American University in Cairo. Dr. Amin is on the board of trustees of the Egyptian Radio and Television Union, the governing body of Egypt's radio and television broadcasting system. He is a founding member of the Arab United States Association for Communication Educators and is the author of many articles and a contributor to several books.

After successful utilization of radio as a means to promote the image of the political leadership of the state, Egypt established its comprehensive television system in 1960.[3] Egyptian television initially began broadcasting its programs on two channels. A third channel covering greater Cairo, added soon after, was banned following the 1967 war with Israel; it was not revived until 1984.[4]

Within the last decade, Egyptian television has instituted a plan to decentralize the terrestrial broadcasting system by introducing local television channels. In October 1988, Channel 4 was introduced to cover Ismailia, Suez and Port Said; the first official broadcast was at the end of May 1989.[5] In December 1990, Channel 5, covering Alexandria and the surrounding areas, was introduced. In May 1994, Channel 6, also known as the Delta channel, began broadcasting. It is currently covering the Delta and the surrounding territories. In October 1994, Channel 7, covering Minia and some parts of southern Egypt, was introduced.[6] Channel 9 covers Aswan and the far southern areas of the state. All of the local television channels are carrying news and news programs on their broadcast schedule for both "target" and general audiences in their local areas.[7]

Visual Language in Oral Culture

Egyptian news is presented using visual content that involves graphics, illustrations, still photographs, maps, charts and video clips. This visual presentation has an information impact on the comprehension and recall of Egyptian audiences. In a verbal culture such as the Arab culture, in which verbal messages are transmitted quickly, rumors are quick to arise and spread and illiteracy is very high, television becomes the most powerful medium of mass communication. It conveys information audiovisually, thereby bypassing the barrier of illiteracy, and adds credibility to news reports.

Visual information presents a wealth of information that, in many cases, circumvents long verbal messages in the Egyptian news. In addition, television news is immensely appealing to Egyptian audiences. Unlike print, it favors movement over stillness, simplification over complexity, specificity over abstraction and the present over the past or the future. Therefore, the power of television news in Egypt relies on the power of the pictures presented in the news. This is becoming the principal issue in television journalism in Egypt.

Government Control and Influence

The Egyptian regime has paid a great deal of attention to television news, promoting the expansion of a government-owned media empire inside the state that could be used as a high-profile tool to form public opinion, enhance public mobilization and deliver the official government line. One good reason for this attention is that most Egyptian households are closely knit and self-contained. This is especially true in the rural conservative part of the state in general, and within the middle and lower classes in particular, where most entertaining is done in the home.

Egyptian officials regarded television news as an acceptable alternative to *Gariedah Misr AlNatiqah* (*The Egyptian Verbal-Newspaper*), a visual newspaper that included pictorial reports about news and events. In the 1950s and 1960s, it was shown in public cinemas before the main movie and was quite popular.[8] Furthermore, state- or quasi-state-controlled television was a means of filtering what viewers saw. At least this was the case before satellite television became popular in Egypt.[9]

The Power of Pictures

Many of the broadcast experts in Egypt have stated the well-known principles that "seeing is remembering," that "one picture is worth (more than) a thousand words" and that visuals are very important to the broadcast news. Visual illustrations on television news are used to increase recall of the news item. Television shows events as they are happening or as they have happened, rather than having to depend on visual descriptions. Visuals are judged not by what they contribute independently but by what they contribute to the verbal text. Pictures are related to the concept of an immediacy in television news that breaks the barrier of time and space and allows us to experience events and familiarize ourselves with people everywhere in the world.

Egyptian television depends mostly on cameramen who lack journalistic skills, although they do have training in fine and applied arts and have artistic skills. When they go on an assignment, they shoot but not to a script; therefore, there is usually a gap between the picture and the text.[10] The lack of journalistic skills in cameramen usually results in improper utilization of the visual language by adding unnecessary camera shots, movements and/or zooming, which confuses the audience and reduces their level of attention. Television audiences do not interpret visuals separately from the text, but instead give attention to the meaning of the entire audiovisual message.[11] News audiences are usually guided verbally by a lead into the meaning and significance of the visual message, with its visuals being largely superficial.[12]

Egyptian television's national news policies reinforce cultural and national traditions and values; any visual content that may cause social confusion or denounce the traditions of Egyptian society is forbidden. Pictures of crime and violence are usually censored. Even the assassination of president Sadat was censored, and, consequently, Egyptian audiences never had a chance to see pictures of this tragedy.[13] One positive action that broadcasters would consider is to ensure that there is a balance of "prosocial" programs showing healthy cooperative behavior, counteracting the harmful, antisocial messages of violent and aggressive images.

Egyptian broadcast news managers state that it is important for the media to understand their responsibilities to their audience and to be more cautious about what they broadcast, keeping in mind that among the audience are children who easily can be affected by what they see.[14] Thus, it is up to the media in Egypt to portray the truth and be objective, especially when portraying events such as terrorist-related stories. The media can easily manipulate viewers into believing that terrorists are brutal and unethical or to show them as "good people." Therefore, they must not abuse this power but, rather, use it in a socially appropriate manner.

Considering how the tremendous amounts of violence viewed on the television news can have negative and aggressive consequences on both children and adults, the broadcast news media in Egypt is urged to be mindful of the visual content of what they broadcast. While they might show the wars, crimes and violence that are going on globally, they are also expected to emphasize the peace, love and harmony found in various societies. Hence, portraying both ends—the good and the evil—is important, rather than concentrating on one and leaving out the other.[15] It is also the role of the government to direct the media as to what to portray, how to portray it as well as how much to portray.

Impact of Censorship Codes on Content

Censorship in Egypt, therefore, is based on broad national and cultural concerns. Within the state of Egypt, censorship is easily tolerated, and even expected as a form of civic responsibility. Some Arab leaders are quite sensitive about criticism; hence, in many cases, the broadcasting of negative pictures of the officers of the state, courts, military and security officers and religious leaders is prohibited.[16]

Arabs have other concerns as well. Many broadcast officials are fearful of the shock of some audiovisual materials if they are presented in the news because they may affect the entire family. Accordingly, rules of censorship of audiovisual materials presented in the broadcast news include the prohibition of any pictures that threaten family ties or condemn family values. In Egypt, as in most Arab countries, broadcasting of programs that include statements encouraging violations of the law, excessive violence or references to gambling or even crime news is prohibited.[17] Other rules include the censorship of any audiovisual materials presented as a news item that favors divorce as a means of solving family problems.

Moreover, news items that encourage discrimination on the basis of color, race, religion or societal status are considered sensitive materials and are also prohibited. Islam, the main religion in the Arab world, forbids the consumption of drugs or alcohol and gambling. Consequently, all Arab news systems censor any content that might encourage the use and distribution of drugs or the consumption of alcohol.[18]

Egyptian officials are also concerned with potential political and religious repercussions from an influx of alien values. In terms of news, censorship has been imposed as a result of the Egyptian government's sensitivity to news reporting by international satellite radio and television networks that is perceived as unfavorable. The lack of skill within governments to cope with what is defined as negative reporting on Arab leadership and Arab governments causes jingoistic responses, such as the banning of satellite dishes in Saudi Arabia, or the refusal to develop telecommunication infrastructures that link Middle Eastern countries with the global information community.

Egyptian television news was brought into the country by the Egyptian minister for information, not by commercial enterprises, as was the case with the print media. Television in Egypt is still an absolute monopoly and under direct government supervision. The medium, since its introduction in Egypt, was owned, operated and controlled by the government. Likewise, television news had, and still has, to a large extent, an information "propaganda" mission and not a journalistic mission.[19]

Much of Egyptian news reporting is focused on protocol news, concentrating on the national agenda of the country and avoiding politically or culturally threatening reporting. Visuals overwhelmingly are restricted to presidential travel, meetings of heads of state and government groups and public events in Egypt. Some consider protocol news that visually portrays the agenda of the country's leadership to be a sort of professional retardation that presents news based on protocol values rather than journalistic values.[20]

The power of pictures is mainly used to show people and events in the capital cities and urban centers in Egypt and the world; visuals are seldom used for people and events in the suburbs and almost never for people and events in rural areas. In this sense, television news is centralized, expressing the desire of the state to show control as well as centralization in the government and administration, leaving rural areas peripheralized.

Television News: Domestic Uniformity

Television news on the two national networks addresses elitist and mainstream audiences that are found in Cairo, the capital city and also the largest city in the country, as well as in Alexandria, the second most populous city. Officials on the main channel know that they are addressing a population of almost 64 million. Although they have an agreement with news wires such as Euronews and Visnews to provide news pictures to the stations, they are not fully utilized. Broadcast experts consider the news slanted, inaccurate, misleading and nonratings-driven.[21]

Even though the state began decentralizing the system by launching a series of local and regional television channels in addition to the two main networks, control of the news remains the same. Local television stations were established in Egypt to address the numerous smaller cities and villages scattered along both sides of the Nile River and in the Nile Delta, but they still depend almost entirely on the main networks for news.

Local television news in Egypt is nonratings driven just like all other television genres in the state broadcasting system. The news is usually perceived by the general population as largely irrelevant, and although it is supposed to allow audiences to see and experience events occurring worldwide, it is generally confined to national news. Because the news is of an overwhelmingly national focus and constrained by its protocol nature, local audiences consider it to be dry, tunnel visioned and unenlightening.[22]

The Start of Global Competition

In the Arab world, international radio news services are very popular and compete for Arab audiences. The BBC Arabic service is rated
first when it comes to radio news. Other rival radio services that play
an effective part in the Arab world include the Voice of America and
Radio Monte Carlo.[23] As for television news, one important consequence of global television news took place when two established
news networks, the Cable News Network (CNN) and the British
Broadcasting Service World Service Television (BBC), launched
international television services. CNN, BBC and Euronews are the
main English language global television news services competing for
Arab audiences in the Middle East.[24] This is in addition to the Arabic language global television news services such as Nile News from
Egypt, the Saudi-owned Middle East Broadcasting Center (MBC),
Al-Jazirah from Qatar and the Syrian Arab News Network (Ann).

In an increasing number of countries, CNN is available via over-
the-air television for most viewers. The impact of CNN in these
"one source" countries, where viewers have previously had access to
only one government-controlled channel, is tremendous. It is perhaps the one place where we can get a substantial quick look at the
impact global news networks might have on the world in the next
century. In authoritarian environments, viewers are exposed not
only to their first international signal but their first alternative to the
national status quo.[25]

One advantage that the BBC had over CNN came when
Orbit Networks, a Saudi-owned satellite operation and the
biggest satellite package in the Middle East, signed a 10-year
contract with the BBC (British Broadcasting Corporation) and its
international news channel, World Service Television, to supply an
Arabic language television news service.[26] This new broadcasting
operation failed when Orbit terminated the contract with the BBC
over a political conflict. The BBC English Language service is now
broadcast on Nile satellite (Nilesat), the region's newest and most
popular satellite source.

CNN: Current Impact

When CNN came to Egypt in 1990, it had a tremendous impact on Egyptian television. In terms of format, Egyptian television began to deviate from the static and sterile voice-over approach in favor of inserting the more dynamic perspective of the television journalist into the news story.[27] Before the introduction of CNN, the presentation of Egyptian television news depended heavily on anchors reading the news for the audiences; visual content was at minimum. Content improved and picture components started to play a role. It was easy at first to do the radio format for television, but when CNN arrived, Egyptian news producers recognized that they had to work on the shape and structure of a newscast. They realized that in addition to the hard news a radio format offers, television's format is much more complex and has time for features, sports, weather and even editorial comments.[28]

The broadcast officials started to pay attention to the television screen and the visual content. One of the most important elements of video journalism is, of course, seen on the television screen as a number of different graphics. The "box" as a visual electronic graphic was finally introduced to the Egyptian news bulletins in the 1990s. This electronic window on the left or the right of the anchor can show maps of the location of a story. Still photographs of people or places or still frames extracted electronically from videotapes—flags, charts, graphs—help connect viewers to the news story.

CNN brought the international standard for presenting news and it was adapted by Egyptian television. The visual dimension to stories began to play an effective role in their presentation, and television interviews have became a more central part of the story. Egyptian viewers began to notice a change in Egyptian television news, and audiences became more personally involved in the story. Television journalism in Egypt had come a long way. Finally, stories emerged from Egyptian television that not only provided two sides to a controversial issue or portrayed issues in a broader context, but also provided visuals that matched the text.

Adjusting to Change

To keep up with CNN's visual content, immediate attention was given to news gathering. Electronic news-gathering and electronic field production systems were better utilized to take audiences where they could listen to people and see national events as they happen; before CNN, viewers were locked into stories by an anchor reading in the studio. A new center for international news, called Markz el Akhbar el Moswara, was created to provide the Egyptian television news media with video materials for their newscasts.[29]

The Middle East now has four competing satellite Arabic news television networks fighting for audience loyalty: Nile News, Arab News Network, Middle East Broadcasting Center, and Al-Jazirah. A few years ago there were no specialized television news networks. The new direct-to-home satellite channels are all free-to-air and enjoy a great degree of freedom while offering a threat to state-run national news, which is usually censored.

The satellite news services are gaining audiences who have started to tune in to this news model. The professional presentation of a broad mixture of news and public affairs programs utilizes the international standard of television news by incorporating high-quality production values that depend mainly on visuals. This new standard has very quickly earned a large and loyal audience.[30]

The quality of the visual content in Egyptian television journalism was sharply declining when it started facing fierce challenges from the global news networks. Although Egyptian experts realize the importance of visual content, it appears—from the official side—that there is little awareness of the importance of the problem of visual language as a priority. Because there are so many international news networks that provide Egyptian audiences at home with accurate visual content and credible, appealing visual language, these audiences are reluctant to tune in to the national news. The gap remains wide.

It seems that the only solution may be to introduce more intensive professional training programs for Egypt's news producers and reporters. One such program is within the Adham Center at the American University in Cairo, the region's only program in television journalism. Professional training is a must for educating those in the news industry if they are to survive the competition from media outside Egypt. A shortage of financial resources and trained production staff is still a common unsolvable problem in the country.

The constant need for visual material on the Egyptian news requires an intensive exchange of news items with other news networks. This is crucial in order for Egyptian audiences to experience what is happening in the world. Finally, the adaptation of new models and formats for news presentation from the major global news networks can break the old static formats and lead to new ways of gaining and holding the attention of Egyptian audiences.

In conclusion, Egyptian television has been able to make a good transition to a more visual news product by implementing the international standard that is being introduced to the world by CNN. However, the best way to achieve excellence in presenting the news is still the challenge before us. The more Egyptians utilize such international standards and improve their production and journalistic values, the better the chances for them to play a larger role in the world news platform. While international networks become more available to Egyptian viewers, they also demand a greater quality of news, more useful formats and a better overall news product that will compare favorably with other international news outlets.

Notes

1. William A. Rugh, *The Arab Press* (Syracuse, NY: Syracuse University Press, 1997).
2. Douglas Boyd and Hussein Amin, "The Impact of Home Video Cassette Recorder on Egyptian Film and Television Consumption Patterns," *European Journal of Communication* 18, no. 1 (1993): 77–87.

3. Hussein Y. Amin, "Satellites and Direct Broadcast Television Services in the Arab World" (paper presented at the Broadcast Education Association Convention, Las Vegas, April 7–11, 1995).
4. James J. Napoli, Hussein Y. Amin and Richard F. Boylan, "Assessment of Egyptian Print and Electronic Media," unpublished report submitted to the United States Agency for International Development, 1995.
5. Amin, "Satellites and Direct Broadcast."
6. Ibid.
7. Hussein Amin, "Arab World Audio-Visual Media," in *Censorship: An Encyclopedia,* ed. Derek Jones (Chicago: Fitzroy Dearborn Publishers, 1998).
8. AbdelSalam El Nadi, interview with former head of television sector, the Egyptian Radio and Television Union, Cairo Egypt, 2 April 2000.
9. Boyd and Amin, "The Impact of Home Video Cassette Recorder."
10. S. A. Schleifer, interview with director of the Adham Center for Television Journalism, the American University in Cairo, Cairo, Egypt, 29 March 2000.
11. Sa'ad Labib, interview with member of the board of trustees, Egyptian Radio and Television Union, Cairo, Egypt, 29 March 2000.
12. Schleifer, interview.
13. El Nadi, interview.
14. Ibid.
15. Labib, interview.
16. Amin, "Arab World Audio-Visual Media."
17. Ibid.
18. Napoli, "Assessment of Egyptian Print."
19. Schleifer, interview.
20. Labib, interview.
21. Hassan Ragab, interview with professor of journalism, Department of Journalism and Mass Communication, the American University in Cairo, Cairo, Egypt, 28 March 2000.
22. Ibid.
23. Labib, interview.
24. Joe S. Foote, "Television Beyond National Boundaries: CNN's Expansion to Egypt." Transnational Broadcasting Studies (TBS), *Electronic Journal* 2, no.1 (1998) *www.tbsjournal.com.* Published by the Adham Center for Television Journalism, the American University in Cairo.
25. Ibid.
26. Amin, "Satellites and Direct Broadcast."
27. Joe S. Foote and Hussein Amin, "Global TV News in Developing Countries: CNN's Expansion to Egypt," *Ecquid Novi, Journal of Journalism in Southern Africa* 14, no. 2 (1993): 153–178.
28. Amin, "Arab World Audio-Visual Media."
29. El Nadi, interview.
30. Ragab, interview.

CHAPTER 8

News on a Global Frequency: Fusing Contrasting Cultures in Radio News

Tony Kahn

I'd like to talk to you a bit about the development of the program that I cohost, called "The World." It represents a mixed parentage as a news show; though it provides you with the news, it also provides you with the news from two very, very different sources. The story of "The World" is really the story of how these two very different resources managed to come together, and sometimes not come together, to create a program for the American listener seeking greater access to international news.

The first resource is, of course, public radio in the United States. Those who listen to public radio, or have listened to it at least once, know that, like millions of other Americans, they can get their news every day from this source far more comprehensively than from TV, or, in many instances, even the newspaper. But, this wonderfully in-depth source of news, called public radio, is really two different entities.

Tony Kahn's extensive career in journalism includes writing, producing, and hosting more than 50 radio and television programs. He is the acclaimed writer and producer of the radio drama "Blacklisted," the story of how his father, screenwriter Gordon Kahn, fell victim to the Hollywood blacklist during the McCarthy years. As host of "The World," an internationally broadcast daily news program, Mr. Kahn interviews leading newsmakers and produces a highly regarded feature segment, "Tony Kahn's Journal." The essay that follows is an edited transcript of a lecture given by Mr. Kahn at the University of Rhode Island in 1998.

The British Broadcasting Corporation—the BBC—is a major contributor of news to public radio in the United States. The BBC is *the* largest news-gathering service in the world. It has nearly unlimited access to everybody and everything that's going on anywhere at any time on the planet. The BBC World Service, which is a division of the BBC, also has a very special history in that during World War II, it was the voice of information and hope for occupied Europe, and, for many of those same countries, after World War II during the Cold War.

One could also say that for many former British colonies, and those might as well include the United States among them, the BBC has always represented the voice of the mother country—it's the voice of the "mother culture." It has those properties that we instinctively respect as authoritative. It goes dispassionately after often very emotional stories. It doesn't get directly involved in the rawer elements of a news event on the street. It relies very heavily on an official policy statement when it analyzes the news and, wherever possible, it tries to stay away from interpreting things on the basis of strong human emotions or the power of the personality.

If the BBC is a beacon, then public radio in the United States is kind of like the campfire—it's the place that provides warmth and light at the same time. It's where educated, thoughtful Americans gather to exchange and swap stories about who they are, and to look at the meaning of the news in far more personal terms.

Another way to look at the difference between these entities is to say that the BBC is like a bulldog, and it will behave like a bulldog in news-gathering situations. If the host of news program, for instance, is interviewing a very important politician and thinks that politician is a liar, you can be sure that the BBC host (they're called "presenters") will challenge that person directly. He or she might say, "Would you like a glass of water to wash down that pack of lies?" BBC presenters will put news makers on the spot!

By comparison, public radio hosts in the United States would be far more likely not to directly confront the person and get the expected "answer": one more lie saying he's not lying. Still, they try to explore what circumstances make it necessary for this person to lie, and what the eventual consequences are for always lying. These are simplified characterizations of the differences between the BBC and Public Radio, but I think they're real ones.

In a sense, one could say that public radio in the States is sort of like the concept of participatory democracy applied to the news. The idea is that the news really doesn't mean as much as it should until you focus on the people behind the headlines, the kinds of cultural contexts behind the politics, the human impulses behind even the most complicated events. The goal is to ensure that people who are listening can see themselves, or understand how they might fit into the story, and understand why people are behaving the way that they do.

People respect the authority of the BBC, and they tend to remember the stories on public radio. There's a term in public radio that I think is very revealing—it's called *driveway potential*. Producers will often talk to each other and say, "We think this story has 'driveway potential.'" What they mean is that when you hear that story and you're in the car, if it's not finished by the time you get home, you're going to stay in the driveway, inside the car, listening to it until it's finished. Then maybe it will also have "kitchen potential." Once you're out of the driveway and you're in the house, and you're in the kitchen, you want to tell somebody what you just heard. You want to pass it on, because it's experience. It's illuminated experience; it makes you feel more alive, makes you feel more in touch with what's going on in the world.

The program that I cohost, "The World," debuted in 1995. It's a daily, hour-long program of international news and international *teachers*: the term we use to describe softer stories, intended primarily for an American audience. It's an attempt to bring these two very different traditions, the "bulldog" of the BBC and the "golden retriever" of American public radio, the beacon and the campfire, together under one roof. Gaining an insight into that process is, in many ways, tantamount to gaining an insight into the cultural differences that define news around our globe.

"The World" is really the result of a partnership among three media organizations: the BBC, Public Radio International (PRI), which is known as the second public radio network (the first one being NPR—National Public Radio—in the United States), and WGBH-Boston. WGBH is probably the largest and most prolific producer of television programming in the public broadcasting system, and was interested in raising its profile as a production place for radio, as well. So, the three of them came together to do the show, in a quest to compete with established radio news programs like NPR's "All Things Considered."

When PRI announced it was going to be broadcasting "The World," the first thing NPR did, for instance, was to make "All Things Considered" an hour long. Then it also offered an entire afternoon programming lineup at a bargain price for stations, so there really wouldn't be much available time for these stations to try out "The World." Despite that, "The World" is heard on 110 stations across the country. It's also on in Europe and parts of Africa and has a daily listenership of around a million people.

"The World" went on the air the first of January 1996. The central concept of this show was really very intriguing, and it was unique. The idea was that the show was going to be built around the worldwide network of correspondents, or "stringers." These correspondents had been born and raised in the countries and in the cultures that they were going to be covering. Unlike outside reporters, the theory was that they'd be able to translate the news for American listeners—not just in terms of its international significance, but also in terms of its local origins and its local impact. They were going to be able to find and weave together the sounds, the music, the cultural trends and just the right human images that are often unique to a specific culture. The goal was to make stories so human that listeners in the United States could immediately identify with them.

At the same time, contributors to the program would be totally avoiding the kind of "foreign-policy speak" and State Department "gobbledygook" that normally is associated with the coverage of international news, and alienates a lot of listeners. So, the idea was that the show was going to demystify international affairs for "real" people by talking about real human events, in much the same way that another show on PRI, called "Marketplace," demystified the world of business by showing that business is really just a very exciting human endeavor.

Our daily hour was going to have a mix of hard news, soft features and background segments called "Explainers." The idea was that people might be a little bit scared the first time they heard that a story was coming from Africa, West Africa, Sudan or other international locations. To counter this phobia, we'd present some stories that would give a context for the story—some sense of where the place is and what its culture is like.

The first and third segments, after a brief newscast, were also going to cover two leading international stories. When you realize that there aren't that many international stories in the whole half-hour on the evening news on TV, this radio show seems particularly remarkable for having four international news stories. Each had on-the-scene reports, and host-driven interviews in Boston and London with the newsmakers: the heads of state, the ambassadors, the spokespeople, the artists. Every show was going to end with a piece of global music, some tune that's a real "hit" in a particular part of the world. There would be something called the "Geography Quiz," for listeners to test their wits, somewhere toward the show's second half.

The London office had all the resources of the BBC right next door, and these resources are incredible. Not only do they have six, seven news wires, not only do they have internal memos going on about what the story of the day is and why, not only can you access the scripts of dozens of programs that are covering stories to see what they said about it, you can also get the torrential output of a network of BBC "listening posts" in several locations. People there tune in to listen and watch radio and television broadcasts—and, for all I know, phone conversations and CB conversations around the world—with the object of covering what the local media is saying about everybody else! So, if they want to know what Peru is saying about Ecuador, or if they want to know how a particular story is playing on some local radio show somewhere else in the world, they can find out!

In addition, London, of course, has a five-hour jump on Boston in terms of what's happening in the world. So, the idea was that London would start by assembling a list of leading world stories. Then when Boston came on in the morning, both sides were going to gather around a conference phone setup. Both sides would discuss the London agenda and determine how it could be tailored to an American audience. And to keep things loose, and to keep people honest, and to keep the editorial spirit global, the editorial lead was going to alternate daily between Boston and London. So, Monday, Boston would have the final edit, Tuesday, London would have it, Wednesday, Boston, and so on, through the week.

Daily discussions took place over which international stories were of importance to the American audience and why. Two examples of the kinds of stories that were discussed back then illustrate the give-and-take that went on in these editorial sessions. The first is a story dealing with the Northern Ireland peace process. This is a story with the potential to make Americans' eyes roll. All you have to say is "Northern Ireland," and you can see the panic entering listeners' eyes. They don't get it. They don't understand it; the history is too complicated. There are too many contending parties; the nationals are more like the partisans and the partisans are more like the nationals. The republicans are the nationalists; the Protestants the Catholics. Which one is England and which one's Ireland? Who's the prime minister of London? Is there a prime minister in London? For American listeners, it's terribly confusing. How much of that kind of background would you have to explain to an American audience every time you mentioned Northern Ireland's problems? Now for the British, of course, there's no problem at all; it would be like a local story. But for an American audience, how much time should I put into the program to get them basically on track?

Let's take the other side of it—what about U.S. stories of global significance? The second Oklahoma bombing trial really didn't play very well in the rest of the world. Well into 1996, it was, obviously, still a very big story in the United States. What if you didn't cover a story that every other news program in the United States was covering? Would your listeners fault you for not saying something about it? Should you try to make a global connection, or should you give up trying? These were the complex journalistic and cultural questions, the complications, that faced us every day from the program's start back in 1996—and still do.

The initial results of our collaboration were exciting and innovative. "The World" seemed to make the world a smaller place. During my first two weeks on the air, I interviewed a homeowner on a satellite phone who was standing on his roof in the middle of a flood in South Africa, describing what was happening, as well as a reporter on a pay phone shouting over a protesting mob that had just broken out of a courthouse in Rome. I spoke to an Iranian official on a tapped telephone in Tairan, who was trying to explain an official position until the other official cut him off. I was talking to an adviser to Yasar Arafat on his car phone as he drove through traffic to an emergency meeting. I spoke to a record shop owner in Tobago, who was talking happily to me on his cell phone in the store's aisle, because he sold out of the first CD by a local Tobago boy who had made good; the CD, by the way, had been produced and recorded in Ontario—one more example of our globally interconnected popular culture. Meanwhile, in our studios in Boston, which were near Harvard's Kennedy School and the Fletcher School of Diplomacy at Tufts, we were drawing so many people of political and cultural consequence for interviews—from U.S. senators to Swedish scientists, to Palestinian ambassadors, to Chinese dissidents.

We did, however, run into a serious incompatibility problem, and it concerned the most distinctive element of the program: the correspondents, or stringers, that I addressed above. Remember, they are the natives of the area that they're supposed to cover; we thought that was a great asset. Theoretically, it *was* a terrific asset. One of the great things about these stringers, I should say, was that they spoke in this wonderful blend of accented English, which really gave the program a distinctive signature sound. You could tune into "The World," and you'd be amazed at how musical English was. It said something about the globalization of the planet. So many people from so many different corners, and so many different walks of life, and each had chosen the English language as the essential means of communication. But they said so many different things! However, that's the good side of the stringers.

The bad side is that they've been trained by the BBC, and their style is kind of dispassionate and official; they try not to get into personal stuff. We, those of us on this side of the Atlantic, were hired, basically, so that we could sound personal. The problem was that they weren't ready to change because they had never been in the American market and really had no chance to experience it, but also because a lot of them came from the BBC. Even though they might not ever be able to advance to the top of the BBC World Service as world-trodding correspondents because they didn't speak with a perfect English accent, the BBC was still their main source of employment. So, I don't think they felt comfortable trying to adapt to learn another style, and a lot of people who were hearing stories by our stringers were saying that that's kind of nice, but I don't remember anything they said! I like the way they said it, but they didn't have a story that could be connected with Americans. They didn't know how to tell stories that we'd listen to.

And there was a difference in their production style, as well, which is sort of an aspect of the BBC style. It was noticeable in the longer pieces that they would do—not the reports on breaking news, but the feature stories, the background stuff. They would take background sound, but they would never use it in a dramatic way. They would always use it to illustrate a point they had already made. Why not pick a sound that's also going on at the same time that might add depth, dimension, to your imagination of the city, or surprise you with some sound you never expected? Or, how about letting us hear what people also like to listen to in the city that helps block out the harsh sounds of the urban environment? What's the music on their Walkmans, or what are they talking about? Is there an argument going on in the background—something that has a human note to it? The stringers often didn't think this approach was appropriate or newsworthy or even correct journalism. So, again, the result was that their thesis might have a wealth of information and ideas in it, but it was often hard to recall what had been said.

In radio programs, as in every other aspect of life, you don't change without a crisis. And toward the end of our first year, it was clear that we had to rethink the broadcast. Everyone agreed that "The World" had to keep its balance of feature stories and hard news, but covering as many as four major, international news stories a day, even if they were the kinds of stories that people might not hear anywhere else, would be a lost effort if the stories couldn't be remembered. If the features were going to run for as long as eight or nine minutes, then they had to have better production, and they had to have a more consistent program style. With people already stretched to the limit, the amount of time and energy spent in daily London/Boston editorial collaborations also had to be reduced.

An hour-long program isn't just a collection of stories—it's a story about stories. In a sense, you're trying to lead people through an entire hour that takes them around the world. For that, you need somebody to organize the material, to figure out why you're covering one story or another, and what the connections may be between them. Sometimes, a 20-second transition that's written for a host to read can be as important in opening a listener's eyes (and ears), as a 4- or 8-minute, well-produced piece. We needed to have the same person, obviously, doing the writing every day so that that style could be developed and so that you could understand what the point of view was.

Despite all this constant evolution, or maybe because of it, the broadcast is making significant advances in some of the areas where we felt we needed to make progress in order to live up to what's expected of a program titled "The World"—a distinctive program, not just another news program. We are providing more political and cultural coverage than anywhere else in public radio about what is happening in the rest of the world. And we are also making sure that we leave no area in the world uncovered for too long, whether or not there is a major news development there. We have a kind of "map," a long list of countries of the world, and there are little blocks running in the other direction for the number of stories we've done in or on that country. By looking at that graph one can quickly determine what parts of the world are over- or underrepresented. Our primary concern lies with making sure that the whole world is represented on a reoccurring basis.

Listeners tell us that the sheer diversity of experiences that we present is important in itself, and that the day-to-day experience spoken in English, in so many different accents, and from so many different places, gives them a growing sense of familiarity with the world and makes them far more willing to pay attention to an event happening in a foreign setting. So, it's not just simply a matter of communicating a story—it's getting past somebody's resistance to even hearing about that story, because the very idea of hearing about it is frightening. The program's challenge is to work on that level.

"The World" is now close to five years old, and that's too young to be wise, but it's old enough to walk and to talk, and to have a mind of its own. And, in these intervening years, the market for international news has changed. Early in our first year, I interviewed Peter Jennings, the managing editor/anchor of the ABC Evening News, and he talked to me about how depressed he was by the incredibly low numbers of stories about international events, and how little interest there seemed to be among the audience. I suspect that if I were talking with him now, his impression would be quite a bit different, if for no other reason than the world really has gotten smaller. Events everywhere do impinge on our pocketbooks, and impact the prospects for our children, and our own futures.

There are many lingering questions about how we cover this "smaller" world in which we all, as global citizens, have a stake. For instance, do you want NPR or PRI to be equal to CNN, or the broadcast networks—in its style, in its speed in getting and reporting the story? Public radio can be seduced by the thrill of a scoop just as quickly as anybody else. Lately, in fact, more and more of the editorial effort of public radio is going to just that. I was talking to somebody recently who was on the news desk at NPR the night they broke the story of what the result was of the second Oklahoma bombing trial verdict; he beat everybody. He said that he was cheered through the newsroom by people who, the day before, hadn't even recognized who he was, even though he had worked there for six months. He said, "Getting there first made me into a hero in the newsroom." Do you feel that the day's most dramatic developments should qualify as the day's most important news?

What constitutes good analysis, or good background, on a crucial development for you, the listener? Do we, or should we, challenge your assumptions all the time about what matters? Should we confront you from a point of view that we think you're not accepting? Are we even asking the right questions? The answers—at least some of them—may reside in how you see the news and what you regard as most important to your understanding of the world.

PART III

Global News and the Reporting Process

CHAPTER 9

Journalism: It's as Easy as ABC

Ted Koppel

I don't know how many of you have ever paused to think about this, but journalism is one of the very few professions that requires no training whatsoever. Clearly you cannot become a doctor or a lawyer without training. You need training to become a carpenter or a plumber. But to be a journalist in America requires nothing more than your assertion that you are one. You don't need a license. You don't have to belong to a union. No permit is necessary. It is a privilege implicitly granted to every American by the First Amendment to the Constitution. Every one of you in this hall here this evening has as much right to call himself a journalist as I do. Until fairly recently, though, that privilege was largely theoretical.

Sure, you've always been able to write anything you wanted; and, for most of this century at least, you could've cranked out a few hundred copies of your screed on a mimeograph machine and then passed them out on a street corner. But if you wanted to reach a

Ted Koppel is the anchor and managing editor of the ABC News program "Nightline." A correspondent for ABC for 17 years before the launch of "Nightline" in 1980, he covered the Civil Rights movement, the Vietnam War, Latin America and the Middle East. For almost a decade, he served as ABC's chief diplomatic correspondent. Koppel has earned, among many other honors, 32 Emmy Awards, 10 Du Pont-Columbia Awards, nine Overseas Press Club Awards, six George Foster Peabody Awards, two George Polk Awards and two Sigma Delta Chi Awards (the highest honor bestowed for public service by the Society of Professional Journalilsts). He is also an inductee of the Broadcasting Hall of Fame and the author of *Nightline: History in the Making and the Making of Television* (1996). "Journalism: It's as Easy as ABC" was the 2000 Red Smith Lecture in Journalism at the University of Notre Dame. It appears in this volume with the approval of Mr. Koppel and the permission of the University of Notre Dame.

somewhat wider audience, you still needed to work for the man (and it almost always was)—the man who owned the printing press.

When I joined ABC News in 1963, there were three networks, and of all the people who watched television on any given day, at any given time, over 90 percent of them were watching ABC, NBC and CBS. If you wanted to work as a television correspondent and reach a national audience, you had to go to work for someone who owned a network.

So it's all well and good, in theory, to talk about every American's right to be a journalist; but for most of the past 223 years, that's all it's been—a theoretical right. That is in the process of undergoing a revolutionary change.

The average U.S. household now receives 57 television channels. That actually sounds more impressive than it is. A lot of those channels are simply reprocessing the programs that used to be on ABC, NBC and CBS 20 or 30 years ago. But there's Fox, there's CNN, there's MSNBC, ESPN, HBO, Showtime, Nickelodeon: all kinds of options that simply did not exist 30 years ago. And they are merely the tip of the iceberg.

The fact is that communicating with a national audience, indeed with a global audience, is now technically within the reach of anyone who can log on to the Internet. And the poster boy of that new reality—indeed, a seminal figure in the new journalism—is Matt Drudge. Matt Drudge embodies the realization of that historic promise that truly anyone in American can be a journalist.

It's not, as I've already suggested, that we lacked the freedom in years past. Most of the time, most American citizens could write or say whatever they wanted. The problem—setting aside, for the moment, political or civil rights considerations—the problem was one of distribution. What difference did it make if I had the freedom to say whatever I wished, if no one was willing to publish or broadcast it? It was journalism's analogue to that old philosophical chestnut about the falling tree in the forest.

Without the capacity to distribute, you could say whatever you wanted, but no one was going to hear it. Now, anyone with access to a computer and a Web site can literally reach anyone in the world who has the capacity to log on. And that's about as technical as this discussion is going to get. Except to add that what any intellectual or idiot can now do in print, either person will soon also be able to commit in living color and on video.

We can already transmit color video over the Internet, and soon that capacity will be routine and nearly universal, which is both a blessing and a curse. But since we're going to have to live with both, I'd like to spend the next few minutes talking to you about consequences: moral, practical, ethical consequences.

To understand the world we're about to enter, you have to know something about the one we're leaving behind. Cambodia, 1970. I want to call my wife in Hong Kong to find out how she and the new baby are doing. You can't call from the hotel; so I hire a cyclo driver to take me down to the PTT, the Post, Telephone and Telegraph. I hand in a written form ordering the phone call; and then I wait— for two and a half hours. When the call goes through, I'm directed to a numbered booth; and when I pick up the phone and say "Hello," I can hear my wife, through a cloud of cotton wool, crackling with static: "Honey, I'm just giving the baby a bath. Call me back in 10 minutes." There was, of course, in those days no way on earth to call back in 10 minutes.

Kosovo, 1999. We are driving, God only knows where, in our armored Land Rover, some miles outside Pristina; and we want to let the office in Washington know what direction we're thinking of taking on a script that hasn't even begun to take shape. This is not an urgent call. This is not a call that must be made. But each of us is equipped with a cell phone that can reach Washington or London in a matter of seconds. We can call our office, we can call our wives, we can call our brokers; we can call to see what's playing at the multiplex on Saturday night. We are linked by an infinite web of strands to a jungle of mostly unessential options.

1970, a beach on the South China Sea. We've just completed an amphibious assault with the Marines a few miles below the demilitarized zone that separates North and South Vietnam, and by the end of that day, I have some sort of a story to tell: about a colonel who insists on water discipline and how, by mid-afternoon, 40 percent of his battalion have been knocked out of action by heat exhaustion because each man was limited to three canteens of water. Anyway, I have this story and it's pretty good; and now I'm trying to hitch a ride back to Da Nang aboard a medivac helicopter. By the time I make it to Da Nang, there are no more flights south that day; but I find a colleague who's flying out first thing in the morning and he'll pigeon the film back to Tan Son Nhut airbase in Saigon for me. Now I spend the next hour trying to reach our office there so that I can tell the bureau chief to have someone meet the flight and transship my film to Tokyo, where it can be transshipped to Los Angeles, where it can be transshipped to New York. There, it'll be cleared through customs by a film expediter, who'll give it to a motorcycle courier, who'll bring it into the lab where the film will be developed. From there it'll be brought into an editing room to be cut and married to the narration that I recorded under a tree, about a mile from the beach where we landed with the marines about three days earlier. And then it'll be screened by one or more producers who'll decide whether they want to use it—and when.

The nature of time has changed over these last 30 years; and with it a wide range of expectations. These days, we would have the capacity to set up a portable ground station on the beach along the South China Sea; and that story of mine that took three days to ship back to the United States, could be satellited back to New York in minutes and on the air as soon as an engineer rewound the tape.

But frequently, these days, we do things merely because we can. The ability to broadcast "live" creates an imperative that simply did not exist 30 years ago. It produces a rush to be first with the obvious; a tendency to focus on events because they "just happened," rather than because of their actual importance. When we knew that a story had to survive for two or three days before it got on the air, we tried to give a broader context to what we wrote. It was pure self-preservation of course; but our stories had to have a somewhat larger meaning than a simple recitation of the latest events. In fact, we learned to leave out the most time-sensitive references because they would date a story, which used to be the surest way to get a story killed.

All too often, these days, news is defined as whatever has happened in the last half hour. And the "live" coverage that is the mainstay of our 24-hour news networks seems to require a constant updating of whatever that day's main story may be, no matter how trivial the latest developments may be. You might think that the accumulation of "updates" would eventually provide some sort of depth; but it rarely, if ever, does. Unless, of course, the main story involves the death of a princess or a Kennedy, the inappropriate-and-absolutely-inexcusable-but-definitely-not-sexual activities of a president; or the progress, along a California freeway, of a white Bronco carrying a Heisman Trophy winner who, it turns out, did not murder his wife. On those kinds of stories, we not only provide depth—there is no end to the depths that we will provide.

What's happened in television news over the last 30 years is completely counterintuitive. Back then, the news divisions had relatively little money (because news wasn't supposed to be profitable), and satellites were few and renting time on them was very expensive. Still, the network news divisions had bureaus all over the world, and foreign news was one of the main ingredients of a network newscast. Now, satellites are ubiquitous and relatively cheap, each network news division has an annual budget in excess of half a billion dollars, and we've closed most of our foreign news bureaus for budgetary reasons. What I'm saying here is applicable to so many different aspects of our lives.

Thirty years ago no one would have bothered trying to reach me on a phone in my car, because car phones barely existed. That may mean that I missed three of four important messages over the course of a year. It also means that I neither received nor made the hundreds of irrelevant phone calls that were never placed because the technology was not yet in place. Now, all too often we do it, not because we must, but simply because we can.

I understand and even appreciate the miracle of e-mail. I have a friend, a doctor, who has given up his practice in orthopedic medicine so that he can satisfy a lifelong dream to sail around the world. No matter where in the world he is, we can reach one another as easily by e-mail as if he were still in his Richmond, Virginia, office. But I am also reached daily, sometimes hourly, by people who feel that simply because they have communicated some banality to me by e-mail (that is to say, instantaneously) that I am under some sort of obligation to reply immediately. I can, therefore I must.

I'm limiting myself this evening to a discussion of communication; and, for the most part, I'll be talking about mass communication, but you know what I mean. It applies to almost every aspect of our lives. Hundreds of time-saving devices should, in theory, have produced a contemplative culture in which we relish the luxury of all those freshly acquired hours. We should be refining the quality of our existence, gravitating toward philosophy and poetry. Instead: "How do I love thee?" I don't have time to count the ways. My beeper's going off. I have electronic mail to answer. My cell phone keeps fading in and out. Direct TV gives me too many options and not enough choices; and television news is becoming a real pain in the butt.

Yes, if a tornado is heading for our community, I am immensely grateful for a television station's capacity to get the very latest information on the air, instantly. But most news stories don't fall into that category. I would prefer, more often than not, that reporters and producers have adequate time to gather their facts, weigh their importance, check their accuracy, align them clearly and elegantly against the video that's been shot.

Journalism is so much more than simply training a live camera on an event. Satelliting back to the United States live video of Iraqi antiaircraft tracers firing into the night sky over Baghdad is a triumph of technology, but it is almost bereft of anything to do with journalism. It is, essentially, a sound and light show, without context. The reporter, attached to his ground station, is required to babble on endlessly, sandwiching guesses between assumptions and seasoning it all with speculation. He could be off gathering information from resident diplomats or even driving through the streets of Baghdad, collecting whatever little nuggets of information can be observed. Instead he is answering desperate and silly questions from Atlanta or Washington or New York, from anchor people whose primary responsibility is to keep the machine running.

Our scientists and engineers have performed brilliantly. They have delivered to us capabilities undreamed of throughout the span of human existence. Where we have failed is in the creation of material worthy of our new media; in the intelligent application of disciplines and standards that acknowledge old verities, even as they adapt to the new realities of an interactive world. A couple of generations ago, T.S. Eliot warned us against the confusion of information, knowledge and wisdom, "Where is the wisdom we have lost in knowledge?" he asked. "Where is the knowledge we have lost in information?" We are, these days, drowning in information, very little of which is translated into knowledge, almost none of which evolves into wisdom.

What Tom Bettag and I have in common with Red Smith is that we all grew up in a world of "gatekeepers," a relatively small community of writers and editors who sifted through the universe of available information and then communicated to its audiences of readers and listeners and viewers what was important or relevant, amusing or entertaining. Not all of these "gatekeepers" applied the best or highest standards, but many did. And among those who did there was a sense of obligation. They had access to information that was, quite simply, beyond the reach of most other people in the world. Competition still gave the process its momentum; the need to boost circulation or attract an audience provided a constant reminder that they were operating in a marketplace of ideas. It was always a moneymaking operation; but there was an editorial process. It was expected that information would pass through several sets of hands, each of which applied commonly accepted standards. Journalism has always been a rough-and-tumble world; but there were certain rules of sourcing and cross checking, standards of editing, language and grammar that always distinguished establishment from tabloid journalism. And somewhere, in all of this, there was an acknowledgment of the need for context. So, what does that say about the expanding world of journalists now operating on cable or satellite TV, and soon to be operating on HDTV or broadband or on the Internet? The glory of those new technologies is precisely that they make the acquisition and the dissemination of information a truly democratic process. As I said at the outset, everyone has always had the right; now nearly everyone also has the reach and the opportunity.

I couldn't possibly reconcile a lifetime spent demanding access to information and the right to disseminate it with now arguing that we should place restrictions on the rights of others to do the same. And anyway, the Internet, in particular, was designed to be immune to precisely that or any other sort of interference. Whether or not Matt Drudge uses two sources or one, (or none, for that matter), is—and should remain—beyond my power to influence.

What I do believe is that the community of professional journalists has a greater obligation than ever before to lead by example. Information on all the media is now so voluminous that it tends toward the chaotic. We can still serve a critical function in bringing order to information.

The new technologies are all geared toward speed. Speed has always been an important part of journalism; but not to the exclusion of other standards. Traditional journalism requires a sorting out of good information from bad; of the important from the trivial. That sort of commitment and expertise may be out of fashion; but the need for it is greater than ever before.

CHAPTER 10

New Wars, New Correspondents

Stacy Sullivan

The world has been shrinking for a long time, but in the 1990s, with the proliferation of e-mail, international commerce and cheap travel, it is shrinking faster than ever before. The result is that faraway places become more relevant to our lives. There was a time when troubles in Indonesia would not have had an impact on our lives in the United States, but living in a global economy, the force of political and economic shocks in Asia reaches all the way to the United States. Today, when we can communicate several times a day with someone in Kazakhstan or Nepal by pressing a button, and when it is not unusual for some people to travel to different continents a few times a year, there is a greater likelihood that events in faraway places will shape our lives.

At the same time, the world has become messier. A decade ago, when the Soviet Union and the United States and their competing ideologies divided the world, international conflicts could always be shoehorned into a communist versus capitalist framework. The new conflicts unfolding around the world, however, are a variety of nationalist, religious and ethnic civil wars that have caught fire in complex, changing and unstable nations—places such as Bosnia, Rwanda, Kosovo and Sierra Leone—that find it difficult to contain

Stacy Sullivan covered the war in Bosnia for *Newsweek* and the Kosovo conflict for the *New York Times* magazine. She is currently a consultant to Harvard University's Human Rights Initiative. "New Wars, New Correspondents" was originally published in the Freedom Forum's *Media Studies Journal* (Spring/Summer 1999), which has granted permission to reprint it in this volume.

135

different peoples in one polity. These conflicts have taken the lives of hundreds of thousands of people and have left millions more homeless and stateless. They have also produced a flood of wrenching and confounding visual images.

But pictures alone do not create understanding—that comes only with detailed reporting on the ground from people who can reconcile breaking news and historical context. And the news media are still obligated to cover distant places. Ethically and morally, it is repugnant to use ignorance as an excuse for ignoring vast regions of the world. Moreover, in an era of great immigration, international stories resonate with a larger number of Americans than is commonly assumed. Finally, for practical reasons, these stories are highly compelling—when they are related by a reporter with enough knowledge of the situation to make them clear.

It would seem logical that as events in foreign countries become both more relevant and more complex, news organizations would expand the number of foreign correspondents and foreign bureaus. Yet with the exception of the wire services and a few major newspapers, almost every news organization in the United States has cut back the number of foreign correspondents and foreign bureaus. The rationale, according to most editors and producers, is simple: Americans aren't interested in foreign news. Moreover, covering foreign news is expensive. It makes bad business sense to spend significant amounts of money producing content that is not popular with readers and viewers. However, because the news media realize their professional obligations to cover these new conflicts despite their complexity and expense, they continue to do so. But not without compromise. Instead of using full-time staff correspondents, almost every American news organization, including the *New York Times*, has come to rely on local hires and stringers instead of staff correspondents to cover the world. Given the complexity, lack of public interest and cost related to foreign conflicts, it is extremely likely that news organizations will continue to do so in the future. I am one of those stringers, and in that sense I represent the future of foreign correspondents.

In the spring of 1995, I graduated from Columbia University's School of International and Public Affairs with a master's degree in international affairs and journalism. During my time in graduate school, I focused on Eastern Europe and passionately followed the breakup of Yugoslavia. I studied the history, politics and language of the region and longed to go there to cover the war. What aspiring journalist well versed in a region embroiled in war would not have felt the same? Were I to have gone the traditional route towards becoming a foreign correspondent—which would have entailed working at a small newspaper, moving on to a midsize paper, then eventually getting a position at a regional or national newspaper—it would have taken a minimum of five years to land an overseas position. That would have put me abroad in my early to mid-30s, just about the time I would want to settle down. Given my interests, my life goals and my expertise in a volatile region, I concluded it made more sense to go to Bosnia, and later Kosovo, while I was eager, single and young.

To my surprise, all of the news outlets I spoke with said they would be open to taking stories from me were I to go to Bosnia. Given what I now understand about the news media's reliance on stringers, it doesn't surprise me, but at the time I was stunned. It seemed a crazy thing to do—run off to a war zone without any institutional backing. But I spoke with several free-lance journalists in the region, and they all assured me that there was plenty of work and that it wasn't that dangerous. It was with those hasty assurances, a borrowed flak jacket and a couple thousand dollars that I made my way to Sarajevo.

Once I arrived, I quickly discovered that there was a gang of free-lancers in the war zone. Among us, we covered the war in Bosnia for *Newsweek*, *Time*, *U.S. News & World Report*, *The Boston Globe*, *The Times* (London), the *Daily Telegraph*, the *Chicago Tribune*, *The Dallas Morning News* and the *Houston Chronicle*—all major news outlets that didn't have full-time foreign correspondents covering the region. All of these newspapers and magazines had staff correspondents, based in Rome, Vienna, Berlin or Warsaw, who would drop into the region from time to time, but the bulk of reporting was left to us—a corps of intelligent and hardworking twenty-somethings who shared a passion for the region and wanted to forge careers as foreign correspondents. The lack of any formal infrastructure from news organizations meant that we had to provide for ourselves. We rented apartments in several different cities in the former Yugoslavia—Zagreb, Sarajevo, Tuzla and Belgrade—and shared the rent. We lent one another cars and shared translators.

It was, in many ways, a mutually beneficial arrangement: the news organizations got an area covered at a discounted rate, and we got to cover a major international story for prestigious news organizations that we could have otherwise only dreamed of writing for. It was also an exploitative relationship that compromised both our safety and the quality of coverage the newspapers and magazines provided.

Not formally backed by news organizations—many of us had contracts, but even these did not obligate the news organizations to give us medical insurance or ensure that we would be evacuated should we get injured—all of us were vulnerable to losing our positions on the whims of editors. We risked being left stranded should something have happened to us. Looking back, I can't help but marvel at how lucky my colleagues and I were that none of us was injured or killed.

Our indispensability to the news organizations, no doubt, was reflected in the coverage we provided. When something particularly newsworthy happened, we found ourselves overstretched, often filing four or five stories each day—recycling quotes and differing each article only slightly. The number of deadlines meant we often had to cut short our reporting time—which no doubt affected the quality of our output. If we had had the security of a news organization behind us and had we been able to concentrate our efforts on one news outlet instead of several, our coverage, and thus that of the newspapers and magazines, would have been substantially more thorough. At the same time, we would not have had to take such substantial risks to our personal safety.

If we were staff correspondents, had anything happened to us, the news organization would have taken responsibility. For example, if I had been captured and detained by the Bosnian Serbs as a staff correspondent, *Newsweek* would have been on the phone to the State Department doing everything possible to secure my release. As a stringer, they did not have that responsibility. What they might have done on my behalf would have been at their own discretion.

Given both the need for more foreign coverage and the economic impracticality of sending more correspondents overseas, is there any other compromise that could be reached that would minimize exploitation and maximize quality and breadth of coverage? I suggest that there is, but the solution requires a new way of thinking about foreign coverage.

The answer is to increase the number of correspondents in overseas bureaus by adding younger and thus cheaper journalists to the overseas staff. The current mentality of magazine and newspaper editors—that future foreign correspondents must move up through the ranks, covering cops and local politics—is inappropriate for the state of a complicated and changing world. The reporting of refugee outflows, mass atrocities and natural disasters is no doubt aided by years of covering local stories—but not nearly to the extent that editors suggest. Regional expertise, experience overseas and linguistic abilities are every bit as valuable as, if not more than, domestic reporting experience.

If those who want to be foreign correspondents—well-traveled people with a talent for languages and an understanding of the complex new world order—had the possibility to get an overseas posting after waiting only a year or two, they would be much more inclined to get a staff job and put in the time it takes to become a staff foreign correspondent rather than taking extreme risks to pursue what they want to do. I know I would have. They would also be willing to earn substantially less than the senior correspondents who currently get overseas positions. And because of the reduced likelihood of younger correspondents having a family that would have to be established overseas, they would cost significantly less to relocate.

In short, editors need to open their minds to a new breed of foreign correspondent—younger, single and, by virtue of the latter two qualities, cheaper than the majority of correspondents currently being sent overseas by most news organizations. That way, media outlets could send more than one correspondent to a region, or keep more than one correspondent in a bureau at marginally higher costs.

If news organizations could increase the number of foreign correspondents in their bureaus, they could also avoid the mayhem and confusion that often accompany big international stories and provide more thorough information to foreign policy-makers as well. Currently, the press ignores many regions of the world until they become catastrophic. Once that happens, correspondents from all over the world parachute in, providing coverage that is erratic and ill informed. Kosovo is a case in point.

The latest battleground in a series of conflicts that have broken out in the former Yugoslavia, Kosovo was an obscure province before it became the biggest story in the world. It was left to be explained by reporters who knew little about it. Yet what happened there in the spring of 1999 was quite predictable.

In October 1998, even as the NATO alliance was threatening to bomb Yugoslavia, most news organizations continued to rely on local hires and stringers to cover the region. I was one of them. As I spoke to people in Kosovo's regional capital, Pristina, I heard the same fears over and over again; if NATO bombs without sending in ground troops, the Serbian population will take out recriminations on the Albanian civilians.

The urban intellectuals of Pristina predicted exactly the events of 1999 in Kosovo, yet very few news organizations reported these fears. I believe this kind of reporting could have swayed policy-makers not to leave the province's Albanian population vulnerable without ground forces or international monitors during NATO attacks, and I believe it could also have saved hundreds, if not thousands, of lives.

Sadly, I have seen the future of foreign reporting—it is Kosovo. I can only hope that the system by which the American news media covers the world will be reformed.

CHAPTER 11

Global News, Changing Views: Economy, Fall of Communism Shift Media Priorities

Alvin Shuster

When I roamed countries in war and peace as a foreign correspondent, I encountered reporters from London's *Daily Express* in every hotel lobby. In Asia, *Le Monde* correspondents were in every village. Just about everywhere, even when the news was less than earthshaking, correspondents from newspapers all over the world gathered, and bad war stories flowed like bad wine, and vice versa.

That still happens at centers of crises, a Gulf War, an assassination, a Bosnia. But the global corps of correspondents, like the world itself, has been changing and evolving, in numbers, style, goals and interests.

To try to determine the extent and nature of these changes, *IPI Report* sampled the state of foreign coverage today and raised a series of questions. Among them:

What has been the impact of cutbacks and recession? How have print and broadcast media adjusted? How much interest is there anyway in foreign news? Has the space and time devoted to foreign

---

A former foreign editor and now senior consulting editor of the *Los Angeles Times*, Alvin Shuster is also the editor of the *International Press Institute Report*. He worked overseas for a decade as a foreign correspondent for the *New York Times*, reporting from Europe, Asia, the Middle East and Africa. "Global News: Changing Views" was originally published in the *IPI Report* (February/March 1996); Mr. Shuster has given permission for its reprint in this volume.

news been shrinking? What are the topics of most interest in various countries?

Some of the highlights of the reports are as follows:

• Print and broadcast media are cutting back on the number of foreign correspondents based overseas, though there are exceptions. With the rising cost of newsprint and of living abroad, publishers took a hard look at those expenses and decided on alternatives such as increased use of wire agencies and stringers and of "parachuting" reporters into crises from home base.

• The collapse of communism has had a clear impact. In Russia, *Izvestia,* which boasted more than 40 correspondents in the "old" days, is now down to 10; *Pravda,* once at 40, now has about 20; *Tass,* once with more than 100, is down to fewer than 70. The tone of the coverage has shifted throughout the former Communist Bloc. Foreign coverage in Russia, for example, has tilted toward moderation with more balanced dispatches plus a dose of the more "bizarre" news from abroad.

• In Asia, newspapers seem to be bucking the trend by increasing their coverage of foreign news, particularly if it is close to home. In part, this is because of the continuing economic boom that has intensified Asian readers' interest in their neighbors. In Japan, the country with the most foreign correspondents, the staff is being reduced in Europe and increased in Asia.

• In Africa, the opposite seems to be true—there is more interest in what goes on in the distant industrialized West than in events on that huge continent. This beyond-the-continent interest is due partly to the links of former colonial powers such as Britain, France and Belgium and partly to the obvious concern about the prices of coffee or copper or gold in Western capitals. Editors tend to rely almost totally on wire agencies.

• In Latin America, editors are experimenting with a new pooling arrangement whereby non-competing papers in Colombia, Argentina, Chile and Peru join in supporting a single correspondent in a newsy capital such as Moscow. "We think it's working," said one editor. "We may try to expand, perhaps to Beijing or Hong Kong."

• And in the United States, newspapers have reduced their staffs at home and abroad, but the major papers that cover the world, the *New York Times, Los Angeles Times, Washington Post* and *The Wall Street Journal,* and the news magazines remain committed to extensive coverage overseas. The television networks have cut way back on correspondents based abroad, but CNN continues to grow and maintains a bigger staff abroad than the major networks combined.

For all the editors in print and broadcast, the new challenge is to try to capture and keep the interest of their readers and viewers. The Cold War is over, the threat of nuclear conflict has diminished and the tendency is to turn inward, to focus more on domestic news and local communities. Bosnia captures attention, as does human suffering elsewhere, but what about the rest of the world?

So much of the coverage beyond national borders, of course, depends on the perspective of the editors and broadcasters making their daily decisions. If they think the public is not interested in international events, then clearly the coverage is minimal, no matter the expense.

It is true that many newspapers in the world—apart from the major ones—do pay only scant attention to foreign news despite the widely held view that overseas developments often have a major impact on domestic concerns. Therein lies the challenge.

"People no longer want to read just news, nude and crude," said Mario Varga, foreign editor of *La Stampa* in Turin, Italy. "We have to give a more behind-the-scenes reportage of political or social events."

"There are very important stories to which we don't do justice," said Christian Malar, foreign news editor of the public television channel France 3. "We don't give enough explanation, enough depth. Coverage stops at pictures and cliches."

Other editors reported that they continue to press foreign correspondents to provide more analysis and insight and to write with a style that will attract readers. Moreover, they are telling their reporters to make their reports more relevant to their readers, to answer the "why should I care?" question.

If the big issue in a country is health care or the criminal justice system, for example, editors say they attempt to look more at how other countries deal with those challenges. And they attempt to do it in a way that will capture the attention of their readers and throw light on complexities.

Long gone are the days when fairly routine news from overseas made the papers, along with the vital and important. In my early days at the *New York Times*, the British budget was played on Page 1 almost every year, no matter its insignificance. Colleagues on other papers broke their backs and expense accounts to get to a coup only to find a counter-coup left things unchanged.

Despite all the changes for the better in the thrust of coverage, frustration too often prevails.

The Munich-based *Sueddeutsche Zeitung*, for example, has lost circulation, partly because of growing unemployment in the area but also because reading habits are changing now that private television has taken hold in Germany.

"We now have people canceling subscriptions because they say the paper is too thick," commented a member of the paper's foreign editing staff, Kurt Kister. "There is an editorial pressure for shorter stories and to reduce costs."

Another problem arises in countries where regimes are determined to shape the way the world is presented to their citizens. This is becoming more difficult in this era of computers and satellites, but the efforts to control the news go on.

The Egyptians, for instance, find balanced coverage of foreign news often hard to come by because so much of their media are linked to the state, which owns most of the news organizations.

In China, newspapers and state-owned news agencies present a broad range of international news. But there are limits, and the government is taking new steps to control the flow of information. Xinhua, the official Chinese news agency, will now supervise all economic news agencies from abroad, which are threatened with punishment if they distribute reports that "slander or jeopardize the national interest" in China.

Economic news, meanwhile, has become increasingly important, and newspapers have been placing a greater emphasis on that coverage. In Britain, the national daily with the largest team of staff correspondents based overseas is the *Financial Times*. *The Wall Street Journal* reports it is expanding abroad. And in Italy, *Il Sole-24 Ore*, the financial newspaper with half a million readers, is the only daily in the nation to keep an office in Tokyo.

So is the foreign coverage all that much better today? The answer is a resounding "yes." Most of the time, it's well-written, informative, important, relevant, analytical, stylish and often bright.

And, to update, the *Daily Express* is now a tabloid with virtually no foreign staff, little coups are no big deal, the British budget still doesn't make Page 1 of the *New York Times* and correspondents now drink a better grade of bad wine.

CHAPTER 12

Business News and
International Reporting

Richard Lambert

One of the most important business stories of the last 20 years was the collapse of the Soviet Union. What seemed at the time like an event primarily of political and strategic importance turned out to have profound consequences for financial markets and businesses everywhere. It transformed the structure of Europe's most powerful economy, Germany, in a way that was to have enormous consequences for all its neighbors. Directly or indirectly, it opened the doors of countries around the world that had previously been closed to foreign trade and international companies. It turned the United States into the unchallenged global superpower and marked the start of a period in which the American brand of capitalism swept across the world.

Here's the paradox. Just as the old model of international news reporting, based on bureaus of general correspondents, has moved into a stage of rapid decline, so the business news organizations have been expanding their networks of specialist correspondents around the world at a hectic pace. While the television networks and big city newspapers were cutting back their foreign coverage and returning

Editor of the *Financial Times* of London, Mr. Lambert is also a highly prolific author in the area of media criticism. His articles have appeared in many publications, including a piece on the news media's credibility, "Rebuilding Trust," in *Columbia Journalism Review* (November/December 1998). "Business News and International Reporting" was first published in 1999 in *Media Studies Journal,* which has given permission for its reprint in this volume.

147

to base, specialist groups like Reuters, Bloomberg, the *Financial Times,* and Dow Jones were—and still are—devoting an increasing share of their resources to global news.

It's not just in the United States that the general public has become more inward looking and less interested in what's happening elsewhere in the world. The same is happening in the United Kingdom and the rest of Europe. It is also true that news organizations everywhere have become more concerned with maximizing profits and less interested in a public service function. Keeping expensive foreign bureaus has become increasingly hard to justify in the face of public indifference.

But in an increasingly globalized capital market, business news organizations have had to move in the opposite direction. As the Soviet collapse showed, political developments can have dramatic business consequences. And economic changes can have an equally big impact on politicians. The collapse of the banking system in Thailand in 1997 caused a chain reaction around the world. It helped to trigger political upheavals in South Korea and Indonesia. It tested the policies of Brazil's President Cardoso almost to the point of destruction. And its reverberations were felt not just in the financial markets of New York, London and Tokyo. They also rippled through the political capitals of the world.

Even the United States, for all its economic and strategic power, has become less immune to economic events outside its borders. International trade is accounting for an increasing share of its economy, and international trade conflicts have become a growing source of aggravation for its policy-makers. U.S. businesses have greatly increased their level of investment outside their own borders, and foreign companies have done the same within the United States. Portfolio investors have been putting significant sums in foreign bonds and equities. And the almighty dollar is facing its first real challenge in decades in the shape of the newly created Euro.

All this is transforming the nature of business news reporting. It is not a coincidence that three of the leading international groups in this area are U.K. based—The *Economist,* Reuters and the *Financial*

Times—because London has been the world's biggest international capital market for most of the last 200 years. But others are now following suite, and business reporters everywhere are having to take a broader view.

For example, the business pages in Detroit in the postwar decades really only had to be concerned with the performance of the big three automakers, which in turn was dictated by their own engineering and marketing skills, and by the strength of the domestic economy. But by the 1980s, these companies were facing serious threats from Japan, to the point where their very existence as volume manufacturers seemed in doubt. By the late 1990s, the story had shifted again. Now the story was about international alliances and takeovers. As Daimler merged with Chrysler, ambitious reporters in Detroit started to think about German lessons—and *The Detroit News* opened a bureau in Frankfurt. In a borderless business world, business correspondents can no longer stop at national boundaries.

Business news organizations need to have bureaus of reporters in international centers for a series of reasons. The most obvious is to cover spot news from important markets. Investors need a running commentary on what's happening in the financial exchanges of Tokyo or London, both because they own shares in those markets and because the way that prices and interest rates move there will influence trading in their own domestic centers. Business readers also need updates on the affairs of the big multinational companies. Who is forming alliances with whom across national borders? How is Sony adapting its strategies to an Internet world? And what opportunities will the deregulation of the telecommunications industry across Europe throw up for U.S. companies?

Business readers are looking for a context to help them understand events in their own marketplace. What is the reason for the prolonged fall in the price of oil, and what would trigger a change? Will the collapse of domestic demand in Japan make its companies a greater threat in international markets, or will it instead blunt their competitive edge? Will the Asian crisis be a good thing for the U.S. economy, by helping to damp down inflationary pressures, or will it pose greater competition for U.S. manufacturers and help to enlarge an already troubling trade deficit?

There are bigger, broader questions that also need reporting from the ground in a way that cannot be done by reporters who are passing through the region on a quick trip. China is the most obvious example. Its political and economic development over the next decade will have enormous implications for international security and trade, all of which will in turn bear directly on the business community. It is a difficult and complex story to report, one that requires an understanding of the subtlety and nuances of politics and culture as well as of the business community. The business news organization that does this best will have a distinct competitive edge and will certainly build its coverage on a platform of strong, locally based reporting.

This emphasis on business as opposed to general news reporting is reconfiguring the landscape of international news. If you drew a map of the world on a scale that reflected the interests of a business readership, the United States would cover more than half the globe. The whole of sub-Saharan Africa might fit comfortably into New Jersey, and you would need a magnifying glass to find Bangladesh.

There are three problems here. The first is that business news organizations have a natural tendency to allocate their resources, both in terms of reporting and space, on the basis of a region's importance in terms of world trade or commodity output. This means that some international stories that are of great importance in strategic terms can get overlooked: Kosovo does not have a natural home on the business pages.

The second is that the priorities of these organizations will change in accordance with shifts in the global economy. In the wake of the OPEC oil boom in the 1970s, the *Financial Times* had a sizeable cadre of reporters devoted to the Middle East. This has been cut back over the years as the oil wealth was frittered away, and more firepower was required in Asia and Latin America. For a business audience, the region is less important than it was. But in terms of human and strategic interest, it remains of vital significance.

The third problem is that stock market movements and international trade flows are not the only guide to the kind of story that is going to matter to the business community, let alone to a broader audience. For example, there is no immediate reason why most businesspeople should care about events in North Africa. For all its natural resources, Algeria has been more or less shut off from the world by its domestic political troubles, and its neighbors to the west scarcely register on the global economic league tables. Yet the political and economic fortunes of North Africa are potentially of very direct economic interest to the whole of Western Europe. If things go badly in the region in the coming years, it is not difficult to imagine a tide of emigration that would pose great social and economic pressures across the Mediterranean.

It takes a longsighted news editor to recognize such issues. Business news reporters are also going to have to learn to ask questions that may not come naturally to people of their background and training. In Europe, for example, there is a broad consensus among the business community that the Economic and Monetary Union is the best way forward. But that view is not so widely spread among the community as a whole—and business leaders do not have a brilliant track record when it comes to judging such essentially political issues. Their consensus needs to be challenged and probed.

Indonesia is another example. Ahead of the economic and political crunch in 1997–98, it was widely regarded by business and supranational organizations like the International Monetary Fund as a model Asian economy, and one that presented great business opportunities. Only later did it become clear that its structure had been undermined by corruption, financial imprudence and human rights abuses.

The growth of global business news reporting helps to plug the gap left by the contraction of international reporting by television and general newspapers. Some publications, like *The Economist* and the *Financial Times* are deliberately seeking to reach out to a wider audience, people who are not naturally readers of business news but who feel the need for a better understanding of what's going on outside their own country. But however successfully they do their job, business reporters in the end are going to be serving a rather narrow and exclusive audience.

One of the biggest challenges in the coming years will be to find ways of keeping the general public in touch with their place in the world. Sound political leadership depends on the support of informed citizens. That in turn requires a steady and consistent view of both local and international events—and one that is not just confined to the business pages.

PART IV

Global News and the Future

CHAPTER 13

Instant News Across Borders: The Computerization of Global Media

Michael D. McKinley

The World Wide Web (WWW) and the Internet have completely reshaped everything we have learned about the average news operation. They have totally shifted the communication parameters. They are available anytime, anywhere—and for today's news organizations, the implications pose a host of unique challenges.

News organizations in the aptly named Information Age face two major decisions. They have to choose whether to remain focused on the old concepts that revolve around public service, or to adopt and embrace the new technology, perhaps even adopting an entirely different concept of journalism.

News organizations also must decide how best to utilize the still evolving technology of new media, which offers a full array of new products and services, new markets that span the globe and the definite promise of new competition. Neither choice offers any guarantees; each strategy requires a careful analysis of potential risks and rewards. Yet, to remain competitive in today's world of multiple

---

Michael McKinley's career in journalism spans more than 20 years, including stints as a correspondent with NBC and CBS. He also has occupied an executive position with the National Association of Broadcasters, where he was responsible for enforcing equal opportunity policies in the broadcasting industry. He has taught at Penn State University as well as American University, and is currently director of undergraduate studies at the University of Phoenix's Maryland campus.

155

choices, successful corporations must encourage their news organizations to provide new and compelling methods of delivering the news.

Most news organizations think that the major benefit of their Internet site is the unlimited inventory space. In an effort to fill this space in what is deemed the most cost-effective manner, many have succumbed to hosting a glut of information that is awash in oversimplification, conflicting or confusing facts or simply "predictions" of news. Many of the news stories on these Web sites focus on war and disasters, or on political and entertainment media superstars, yet they lack the highest standards of artistic skill or statistical accuracy. In fact, much of this so-called cybernews is nothing more than what I would call "sitcom journalism." It is transferred into cyberspace directly from TV, radio or print news-gathering operations.

Yes, we can read, listen to and view news reports from around the world on the WWW from a host of U.S. media companies, owing to the new audio/video streaming technology. But even with the increased inventory space available on these sites, very little international news is to be found on most U.S. media Web sites. Today, not even sites for CBS, ABC, NBC, CNN, NPR, the *New York Times* or the *Washington Post* provide a fraction of the international news available for coverage. What news we do find on these sites is covered in terms of what the story means to Americans.

In fact, an informal survey of many of these cyberstories reveals that they often contain the language "State Department reaction" or "White House reaction." The link between events around the globe and repercussions here in the United States is rarely made by journalists and constitutes a serious oversight on the part of these media operations. This lack of interest in international news stems, of course, from the apparent indifference on the part of Americans to the world around them. Yet, the opportunity exists for news operations to deliver international news that educates the public, by linking global news to the effects this news has on local residents and the global community as a whole.

The simple truth is that there is a multitude of television, radio, magazine and newspaper Web sites. They offer us an abundance of news and information choices. But few are maximizing their efforts to do what they could to inform the public about global events. For example, little has been done to spread the word about the number of children who have died in Iraq as a result of U.S. economic sanctions. The history, context and background the public needs to understand the implications of these sanctions are readily available to journalists, but for the most part, they are not a function of today's headlines in the U.S. media. They are found neither in their over-the-air broadcasts, nor on their Web sites.

An international incident that began early in 2000 caught the attention of not only the citizens of the United States, but also of the world. A young mother tried to escape the political state of Cuba and brought her young son, Elian Gonzalez, with her aboard a boat headed for the U.S. shores. The boat capsized, and the mother succumbed, but the young boy was rescued and brought to relatives in Miami. The young boy's father was not aware that his son was being brought to this country and wished to have him returned. While our government officials and those in Cuba were in daily debate over the fate of this young child, the citizens of the United States were verbal in their opinions.

Should the boy be returned to his father, returned to a Communist country where he surely will not have the same rights and privileges he will receive here? Or should he be kept in the United States, against the will of his father and his country, in the best interests of the child? These were the questions asked, and they highlight the necessity for global information. How many of us, when voicing our opinions, honestly knew the conditions this young boy would bear, should he stay or return?

Here was one example of an opportunity for the media to use the old and new technology to further enhance cocultural communication. MSNBC, the NBC-Microsoft cable network, to its credit, recognized the importance of using the technology to better our understanding of this case, and gave daily, in-depth coverage of the issue and all its ramifications. The public was informed, educated and involved.[1]

The public has shown they have a growing interest in health, education, finance, government regulation, the environment and news from all corners of the globe. The U.S. media has an opportunity to satisfy this interest by using Internet technology to sort out information and news by topic—be it local, regional or international—and to archive it, allowing users to retrieve information when they choose. For the first time, news and information can be accessed by the consumer either in the conventional method, viewed in a traditional broadcast time frame, or in a new definition of news, on demand.

The 21st-century technology of the WWW is not a mass medium like traditional media—local radio and TV, network TV, news publications and newspapers. Instead, it is more of a niche medium, where users search out and pay attention only to those sites that are of interest to them. The Web offers unique opportunities to create a new form of interactive online communication within the global community.

Cyberjournalists and news organizations have an opportunity to reach the Internet generation using still-emerging methods and techniques. With e-mail, pagers, laptop computers and mobile phones, the workplace is no longer confined to one location. It is pervasive. The virtual office never closes. The demand for content does not acknowledge specific hours. This offers newscasters the potential to satisfy a news audience, anytime, anywhere. The potential exists for news that is vitally important to virtually anyone, anywhere in the world.

There is a misconception among some broadcasters that their Web sites are simply an extension of their "brick and mortar" operations. Yet, what we are discovering is that the audience that visits a Web site differs in many ways from the traditional over-the-air audience. The Web site visitor can choose from literally millions of sites and can stay on each site as long as he or she wishes. The sheer volume of material and information offered online coupled with the ability to selectively choose among the most narrowed and focused content means that only those sites that provide what the consumer sees as valuable will reap large online audiences. By nature of the technology itself, the average online visitor has reached both a higher educational level and a higher income level. Online visitors' interests are apt to be more global and yet more self-directed. In the news business, that means they may have a more than average interest in global news, economy and world affairs.

This can also be a boom for online advertisers, when it is realized that the audience that is viewing their advertisements may be targeted in a much more direct manner, and the results of their advertising tracked in ways never before dreamed of. The beginning of interactive advertising, as seen in Europe today, will bring about even more widespread changes in the delivery of content.

Imagine seeing and hearing the latest news story from Europe, having the ability to search the archives for additional background on the subject, complete with audio and video streaming, and then with one simple click of your mouse, remote control or button, you are able to purchase the article or book that relates to this news subject. Think of the ramifications when the audience can use the Internet to turn to the latest stock market report in China and, again, with a simple click, trade their own stocks directly from that site. For the first time, the news viewer will actually become a news maker, because the public's actions will have an immediate effect on the outcome of the story.

News sites can offer interactive areas that allow users to poll their opinion, participate in a survey, leave comments and even make purchases. Each of these extra features requires additional elements behind the scene to make them effective. Obviously, it makes sense to develop partnerships with companies that are astute in these areas, rather than try to develop entirely new departments within the parent news company.

The success of the Internet is proving to be tied to partnerships, even though some studies have shown a high failure rate among some of these newly forged relationships. These alliances appear to be working because they allow the participating companies to achieve cost savings through economies of scale, and they allow one or both companies to have access to the other's proprietary technology. But, of course, the key concern for such alliances is how both companies stimulate growth and make money with their partner.

Partnerships on the Web are prevalent in industries with rapid change such as media, entertainment, biotech and high tech. Such alliances bring together many different kinds of organizations and companies with various types of management and operating structures. Management experts claim that it is no longer *whether* to create a joint venture or alliance but *who* will be the appropriate partner. As the technology develops, so do the providers of entirely new businesses to support the new business model.

The necessary elements or functions of the successful news site are still evolving. The possibilities are endless. Traditional over-the-air broadcasting is limited by time; there are still only 60 seconds in an hour, 24 hours in a day, but a news operation's Web site has unlimited inventory. Designers can add as many pages and hyperlinks as deemed worthy by management. But to provide timely and current content for both of these areas—broadcasting and the Internet—is a hardship most news operations cannot or will not overcome alone. This is the area where partnerships are valuable.

Let us look at the areas that may be of interest to the average online news viewer, beyond traditional news stories. We can add news about the economy, adding overseas and national stock prices, graphs, tracking and research. This area can be interactive, allowing visitors to open their own "account," track their own personal stocks, and make transactions 24 hours a day.

Other areas of successful partnership, specifically in the news and journalistic fields, include the delivery of weather, traffic, health, education and additional resource information. As you can imagine, it is beyond the ability of any one organization to gather and deliver the vast amount of content needed to keep these areas current.

In addition, many sites offer added features to provide visitors with more reasons to return again and again. This is called making a site "sticky." The goal of a media delivery site is the same as that of a traditional broadcast or publication. One must gather as many readers, viewers and visitors as possible, to make that site attractive to advertisers.

Excellent examples of these complex partnerships include the 1996 merging of Microsoft and NBC's broadcast network to operate the all-news channel MSNBC along with an online cable Web site to operate in conjunction with NBC's network. America On Line (AOL) fueled its growth in early 2000 by teaming up with media giant Time Warner to form a partnership between the site with the most "eyeballs" (viewers on line) and the corporation that controls a wealth of content. AOL is aware that the way to win the Internet strategy competition is to provide the most people with the information they want most.

According to Susan Pickering, Media Consultant for Global Media Corporation, "Content will be the deciding factor in the success of tomorrow's Web sites. We have built the consumer's expectation to include both immediate response and unlimited content. In order to build and maintain a site that is *sticky*, or one that users will revisit and spend time on, the content must be compelling, comprehensive, and fresh."[2]

Pickering also states: "It is impossible and unreasonable to expect one company or organization to be capable of fulfilling this enormous task alone. Just as newspapers print information from many outside reporters and sources, just as television adds clips from outside sources, so must Web site managers look to outside partnerships to gather content. The goal is the same: 'Superserve' the user; bring as many eyeballs and ears to the site as possible."[3] The Internet user of today and tomorrow has many choices at his or her disposal, and users expect to find what they want, in as much depth and detail as they choose. The ability of today's online journalists to develop meaningful partnerships with those who can provide valuable content to their sites will be the backbone of the successful Internet business model.

Kenneth Gamble, an online news producer for WRC-TV, also known as NBC/4, the NBC-owned and operated television station in Washington, D.C., agrees. "We have a mission to be as profitable as we can. But we have another mission. And that's to be the pre-eminent leader in news coverage. We want people to come to NBC/4, when they log on their computer or turn on their television. We want people to think of NBC/4 as their authoritative news source."[4] Gamble says the station has assembled a team of three people whose job is to tell stories on the Internet that have an interest to people in the Washington, D.C., area.

WRC-TV is one of a small but growing number of stations and networks that provide some of their news programming via the Web. Any consumer with a high-speed connection to the Internet (called broadband) will find television and radio (video and audio programming) increasingly integrated into their online experience.

As digital television and broadband services continue to evolve throughout the decade, this integration will become increasingly seamless and ubiquitous. Again, it is important to note that WRC and the 400 or so other TV stations that maintain Web sites produce local content. There is very little international news.

Three elements are primarily responsible for driving these business partnerships in the information age:

1. *Regulatory approval.* The federal government has taken note of a new global business model and has issued new guidelines that encourage procompetitive collaborations.
2. *Global competition.* More interrelationships are forming as foreign markets rapidly open their markets to information technology and accept multinational companies that are anxious to push into new markets.
3. *The economy.* As Internet business models become larger and more complex, both large and small companies recognize the importance of partners to share the risks in cost, research and development. As Internet business models evolve, the possibility of success as a stand-alone venture has diminished.

The Internet and Web technology offer the consumer, in this case the general public, more flexibility, but access to the technology still presents another major challenge. A July 1999 U.S. Commerce Department report found that between 1997 and 1998, the gap in

Internet access between those at the highest and those at the lowest income levels in our country grew by 29 percent. Whites are more likely to have access from home than are African-Americans or Hispanics from any location.

As technology continues to spread, we must question the effects it will have on our society. Can we balance the benefits with the losses? For we do experience loss. As we encourage more electronic communication, we can fall victim to disassociation. No longer can we be sure that there will be a human voice at the other end of our communication.

We are in the shadow of information overload. Just as the new technology can offer instant information, so it delivers constant interruption—cell phones, pagers, electronic mail, satellite-delivered messages and programs, anytime, anywhere. What is the effect on social relations? Work, after all, is more than just a job or paycheck. It is a community within itself, where we meet friends, share ideas and build a common sense of purpose and a social network.

With the emerging acceptance of voice mail, e-mail and computer networks, how do we preserve the human network and the social interaction that the workplace has helped to facilitate? Can we find a way to harness this new technology to enhance our engagement with others in the world? The possibilities exist to use this technology as a tool to educate and inform. It can be used to overcome the public's lack of information about the world beyond our borders. But it is still unclear whether it can overcome the public's indifference.

Notes

1. A. Mitchell, K. Sanders, J. Avila, "The Elian Story," The Associated Press, Reuters, 6 April 2000 *http://www.msnbc.com/news/386305.asp#BODY.*
2. Susan Pickering, telephone interview, 2 February 2000.
3. Ibid.
4. Kenneth Gamble, personal conversation, NBC: Washington, D.C., 24 March 2000.

CHAPTER 14

Rapid Access and the News Consumer: Ethical Aspects of Today's Technology

Tony Silvia

He may not be the person whose name and face we hope to see when the next generation of journalists or academics write the history of our craft. He is not among those people we hold up to ourselves or our students as role models. He has become, in a sense, the symbol of putting process before thought, action before reflection. His name is Matt Drudge, and, although there are those who despair of even placing his name in the same sentence with the word *journalist*, there is every reason to believe that the concept, if not the execution of global news gathering and reporting, changed irrevocably in 1996, when his "Drudge Report" disseminated the story of President Bill Clinton's then-alleged infidelities with a White House intern named Monica Lewinsky.

It wasn't that the story hadn't been printed elsewhere; it had. But Drudge was the first to disseminate the story widely to a mass audience, both directly and indirectly. The story "broke" on his Web site, of course, but had it remained there, viewed by a relatively few readers, one can only speculate if the history of the United States might have taken a different course, if indeed Bill Clinton would have ever been confronted at all with the allegations leading to his near expulsion from office. Drudge, if he even remains more than a footnote in journalism or media history, will remain so because he, in a sense, changed or expanded the rules of the game. That game is rapid

165

access to information, both for the news consumer and for the news practitioner.

Lawrence Grossman, the former president of NBC News, has called what Drudge symbolizes "the high decibel ricochet effect of today's non-stop multimedia environment."[1] NBC's Tom Brokaw, quoted in Grossman's essay, calls the same phenomenon "the Big Bang theory of journalism." It's not that Drudge himself was the sole or even the primary messenger of the Clinton-Lewinsky scandal; he didn't even break the story touting the existence of a semen-stained dress—ABC's Jackie Judd had that story before Drudge. The name now synonymous with "Cyber Gossip" made his mark because the mainstream media helped validate his message and his story. Grossman points out that soon after the story appeared in the "Drudge Report," the so-called mainstream media organizations—NBC, CBS, ABC, and even the *New York Times*—began repeating the Drudge drumbeat, to audiences that far and away exceeded in size any readership that Matt Drudge himself could ever have imagined.

I would argue that the rapidity of the information and the ease of its availability on the Internet created a situation in which journalists in so-called legitimate newsrooms across the globe, but especially here in the United States, became so seduced by the story's marketability that they became blind to its source. At the point where Drudge was paraded before NBC's large and lucrative morning audience, NBC, Grossman points out, had "done none of its own reporting on the story or gotten any independent verification."[2] Instead, NBC relied on the Internet and one of its chief gossip brokers for its sole verification. Why? Because the technology had made it so easy to access the story, so economically advantageous, that it was tailor-made for the 24-hour news cycle that demands to be fed.

As Grossman points out, the major networks could bring Drudge on programs like "The Today Show" and solicit the information from him, absolving themselves of the need or the obligation to do any substantive reporting or research of their own. In the bargain, they might even avoid litigation if the story turned out not to be true. After all, they were only quoting a source. And the nature of that source, a minion of the new technological age, that vast frontier we call the Internet, must have seemed particularly immune from the kinds of scrutiny that most sources undergo. The Internet is, at best, an ethereal entity—here today, gone tomorrow; much like the technology that created it, it is constantly evolving. So, too, it would seem are the guiding standards or principles that traditionally accompanied slower forms of information dispersal: the printing press, teletype wire or film camera.

It is important to keep this perspective in mind: Without the Internet there could never have been a Matt Drudge. Without the technology, he could never have gained access to a national or international forum. On the other hand, without the technology, that same forum could never have gained access to a Matt Drudge. He would never have created the brand of awareness of himself or his story that would lead to the international stage on which he became known. Put simply, Matt Drudge in himself is not as important as the means he used to create and replicate his message. The technology of the Internet is a technology that creates expectations at the same time as it scuttles to satisfy them. Its rapidity is part of a media culture in which rapidity has replaced reflection. Rapid ease of access to information has put certain stories and categories of stories on news managers' agendas that, minus today's technology, might not have entered our collective journalistic consciousness.

There is no argument that many of these stories are important ones, with strong consequences for our world. No one could argue, for instance, that rapid ease of access to information about Bosnia or Kosovo is a positive outgrowth of Internet technology. But, equally, it would be hard to argue that much of what is processed as news in this new technological environment is trivial by comparison: news of the latest celebrity breakup, makeup or movie makeover, for example. Although the technology has made it possible for us, as citizens of the globe, to be more informed about more aspects of more cultures, the reality is that most Americans still are unable to locate Bosnia or Kosovo on a map. The rise of technology alone would not appear to be enough to better inform our readers and viewers. It empowers us to do many things using vast bytes of streaming audio and video. But does it make us better journalists, improved brokers of honest information? Or, does it, in many ways, work against that process?

The Internet is hardly the beginning, nor will it be the end of the advanced technology that makes the journalist's job simultaneously easier and harder—easier because it makes information processing and transmission tantamount to child's play, harder because some would argue that this same technology complicates the decisions we make about what gets covered and what doesn't. The supposition was once that these decisions had to be made due to a paucity of space and airtime. The Internet, of course, has changed the dimensions of what we once called the *newshole*. Once that term was used to describe a finite space of column inches or minutes in a newscast. Today, it is seldom used, the concept nearly obsolete. As a result of an infinite amount of space available online, editors no longer are compelled to eliminate one story in favor of another for the sake of time or space. Still, the editorial process requires that content decisions be made. It's the criteria for making those decisions that have changed and will change in the future.

Ted Koppel, in an address to a college audience (reprinted in this volume), stressed that the Internet is just one part of an overall societal imperative toward technology at all levels: a world filled with cell phones, pagers, laptop computers and palm pilots. He recounts how, as a young correspondent, there were many stories he wrote in the heat of the moment that never saw airtime. The year was 1970 and Koppel was reporting from Vietnam. Having written his story, he had to hitch a ride on a medivac helicopter to DaNang, find a colleague who could fly the film to an airbase in Saigon the next morning, arrange for someone to meet that flight and get the film to Tokyo, where it could be shipped to Los Angeles, where it would next be shipped to New York. There, it had to be cleared by customs, brought by a motorcycle courier to a lab for processing, sent to an editing room to be cut and matched to the recorded narration and then "screened by one or two producers who'll decide whether they want to use it . . . and when."[3]

Koppel's point is that back then, 30 years ago, publishing or broadcasting a story took *time*: time to research, time to write, time to record, time to transmit the final version to an audience accustomed to waiting for their information. Along the way, there was always the possibility that judgment, the reporter's own or that of an astute editor, could intervene and pronounce a story trivial or, at the very least, less important than it at first seemed. Considering the many hurdles that had to be jumped, the correspondent himself or herself might decide that the story just wasn't worth it. By contrast, in today's 24-hour news cycle, publishing or broadcasting a story is just a mouse click away. As Koppel observes: "The nature of Time has changed over these last 30 years; and with it a wide range of expectations. These days we would have the capacity to set up a ground station on the beach along the South China Sea; and that story of mine that took three days to ship back to the United States, could be satellited back to New York in minutes and on the air as soon as an engineer rewinds the tape."[4] Judgments of significance or triviality are often sacrificed in the name of speed.

This has had a profound impact on both the journalist and the audience. In one sense, deadlines no longer exist. There is no necessity to hold a story until 6 p.m. or for the morning paper, simply because you may not have all the facts or visual images until then. In another sense, deadlines never cease. The technology has made it possible, even inevitable, for news managers and audiences to expect all that we, as journalists in the field, know *now*. The problem is that often we don't know very much about a story, particularly in its early stages. We cannot always adequately judge its immediate impact, let alone its long-term relevance. Despite that, Koppel told his student audience that reporters in the field are constantly implored by their editors, on cell phones at a long distance, to assess, appraise and anoint a story as a story, often long before it has fully developed: "The ability to broadcast live creates an imperative that simply did not exist 30 years ago," he stated. "It produces a rush to be first with the obvious; a tendency to focus on events because they 'just happened' rather than because of their actual importance."[5] He suggests that this can lead to many stories that are, at worst, nonstories being thrust into public view. The infinity of the newshole demands it, the audience expects it and the technology makes it possible.

If news in the 21st century knows no deadlines, it also knows no boundaries. Due in large part to the elimination of technological barriers, geographical borders between nations have also been minimized. The entire concept of "global" news, in fact, might be called a function of this new, borderless terrain. Cyberspace affects more than a nation's computer systems. News in cyberspace has the potential to impact that nation's culture. Governments and regimes can no longer prevent information from reaching its citizenry. For example, in 1996, the Serbian government imposed a news blackout within its borders on war-related information. As the *New York Times* reported, the blackout was to no avail; the technology of the Internet made it possible for Serbs to learn about what was going on inside their country from sources outside their homeland. As the *Times* observed: "When President Slobodan Milosevic, faced with large anti-government demonstrations, tried to shut down the last vestiges of an independent news media last week, he unwittingly spawned a technological revolt he may soon regret."[6] The *Times* reporter went on to outline how "tens of thousands of students, professors, professionals, and journalists immediately connected to Internet web sites across the globe."[7] Even in nations where there is neither a First Amendment nor free speech, technology has made access to outside sources for news facile and immediate.

Satellite technology has made it impossible for dictators and demagogues to keep their political agendas secret from the rest of the world, as well as from their own peoples. Thanks to the satellite receiver dish, CNN is seen in every nation on earth, and its all-news progeny, MSNBC and Fox News Channel, are being beamed into fewer, but still a significant number, of homes globally. Carla Brooks Johnston's study of global television news reveals that Rupert

Murdoch's STAR television service provides news and information to 173 million viewers who receive free access in 40 countries, among them China, India, Taiwan, Israel, Saudi Arabia, Hong Kong, Thailand, Pakistan and Kuwait.[8] Murdoch's SKY TV is in South Africa as well as Europe. Visual equivalents of the long-standing global transmissions by the BBC World Service on radio, these networks give nations the ability to watch each other during times of peace and in times of war. The omnipresent satellite dish transmitter, used by reporters in the field, has had a profound influence on this process—especially during wartime.

As the Persian Gulf War showed, the speed of information transmission by the news media has long since surpassed the Pentagon's ability to keep up. Who can forget the comment by high-ranking Army brass that they first learned vital information relating to the success or failure of a given mission not from their field commanders, but by watching CNN. I once spoke with a U.S. army colonel who confirmed this scenario. "I could be at my command headquarters less than a mile from the site of engagement," he said. "I could hear the bombs exploding and be in radio contact with my battalion." Still, he added that he could often learn the result of the battle faster on CNN than from his own intelligence in the field. Technology has become so advanced that there are no barriers news professionals cannot cross—even those on the battlefield.

The fact that journalists have at their disposal all the technological tools to render deadlines obsolete and borders permeable begs the question, Should they, in every instance, use these tools? As the late Fred Friendly, former CBS News president and colleague of Edward R. Morrow, was fond of saying, just because we *can* do something doesn't mean we *ought* to do it. In today's global news arena, that means the ethical dimensions of news decision making cannot begin to be addressed by the technology of news processing. The difference has become increasingly apparent ever since that first "Drudge Report" found its way onto the mainstream media. "Processing" a Matt Drudge for the "Today Show" is a technical function; questioning that process is a function of judgment and perspective: the domain of the journalist, ripe with what Ted Koppel calls "moral, practical, ethical consequences."

The technology available to today's reporters and editors has led to a rush for instant meaning in stories in which the actual meaning may come at a distance of weeks, months, even years, if ever. But the technology possesses a seductive immediacy that creates in both journalists and audiences a new standard for what is news and what is not. Reporters filing a live report from a far-off land either must have immediate answers to complement the immediacy of the technology or pass up a story in favor of one that can be told simply and quickly. This becomes, yes, an editorial decision, but does it not also have ethical and moral ramifications? How is the audience for news and information in America best served by a report that suggests facile answers to complex problems? How are audiences in nations outside America served by stories suggesting that Americans actually have simple answers to complex political and societal dilemmas? Do both audiences, American and international, receive a skewed version of reality that creates or reinforces certain nationalistic stereotypes? Where technology breeds distribution, it can create distortion.

In discussing television coverage of the Columbine school shootings, Ginger Casey observes that "the search for instant meaning has resulted in a rush to facile judgments. Rap music takes the rap for inner-city violence, Marilyn Manson and video games are blamed for setting off troubled teens." And, for those both inside and outside America's borders, same-day, indeed same-moment, coverage of such a story reveals an instant news menu where "liberals blame guns, conservatives blame culture, religious leaders blame family values or lack thereof."[9] The theories behind what caused the shootings may contain some truth, but they are, at best, frustrating attempts to answer the journalist's mantra "why"? They are the most obvious method to capture sound bites that can be transmitted instantly around the nation and around the globe. The ethical dilemma enters, as Casey observes, because "figuring out what ignites someone's emotional fuse is a complex process that does not readily lend itself to sound bites." Journalists and audience alike, hungry for the rapid answers technology promises have become "a nation of global rubberneckers who pull up to the TV to have momentary connections to the world, connections we can sever with the click of a remote."[10]

One could deduce from a ranking of 1994's top news stories by the U.S. editors of the Associated Press that such connections to the world are indeed temporal. Although the survey includes choices of the genocide in Rwanda and the U.S.-led mission to Haiti, and Palestinian self-rule in Gaza and Jericho, the editors ranked each of these stories in the bottom 5 of 10 choices. The top five choices included O.J. Simpson (#1), labor troubles in baseball and hockey (#3) and the Tonya Harding-Nancy Kerrigan imbroglio (#5).

This may tell us something about the parochial nature of American journalists or about their perceived need to attract and retain a parochial audience. More likely, it says a great deal about how each of these stories plays to the strong visual, the facile sound bite and the simple solution. Each can be understood and transmitted globally in a matter of minutes, not hours or days. When the next reality is a click away, murder, mayhem and money seem a fitting use for our instant technology. Speed and simplicity take precedence over importance.

This is not to suggest that speed is a bad thing. Koppel points out that it has always been an important part of journalism, but "not to the exclusion of other standards." Traditional journalism, he says, "requires a sorting out of good information from bad; of the important from the trivial."[11] Perhaps that, after all, is what the audience is trying to tell us journalists.

In a *Columbia Journalism Review* poll of 125 journalists taken soon after the Bill Clinton-Monica Lewinsky story, only 1 in 10 said they would change the way they cover public officials' private lives, and the vast majority—55 percent—gave their profession high marks for its overall coverage.[12] On the other hand, polls show that some 60 percent of the public shared the perception that the news media were anxious to bring down a popular president, a fact that Richard Lambert calls evidence of "a disconnect between newspeople and their readers and viewers."[13]

Although the polls don't address this point, it is possible that Americans aren't atypical of readers and viewers across the globe. They may watch the sordid sound bite, read or listen to the sleazy details, and they do, but they also don't mistake what they have just seen or heard for news. It becomes, instead, the rapid, technological equivalent of fast food. A Roper Center poll indicates that Americans use words like *right* and *wrong* when discussing news coverage, indicating a level of longing for some measure of ethics from those who give them their news. An astonishing 87 percent also say they are interested in worldwide news.[14]

Each of these findings ought to serve as a reminder that the news audience isn't nearly as hypnotized by the technology as journalists often are. In the final analysis, what they want is to trust in the judgment of those who bring them the news and no amount of whizbang will substitute for that trust. In 1998, Pope John Paul spoke of that trust in a message to journalists. He stressed the need for greater responsibility in this age of the Internet and other rapid transmission systems. As quoted by Grossman,[15] he called on journalists to "transmit information while respecting truth, fundamental ethical principles, and personal dignity." Ironically, in one form or another, these are all elements of one of the oldest codes of ethics in journalism: that of the Society of Professional Journalists. And today that information is even online, rapidly accessible to all journalists everywhere. In less than a millisecond, its influence could reach far beyond that of even Matt Drudge.

Notes

1. Lawrence Grossman, "Spot News: the Press and the Dress," *Columbia Journalism Review* (November/December 1998), 35.
2. Ibid.
3. Ted Koppel, "Journalism: It's as Easy as ABC." The Red Smith Lecture in Journalism, University of Notre Dame, March 2000, 9.

4. Ibid.

5. Ibid.

6. "Serbs Go On-line After Media Blackout," *New York Times,* 11 March 1996, B-1.

7. Ibid.

8. Carla Brooks-Johnston, *Winning the Global TV News Game* (Boston: Focal Press, 1995), 93–94.

9. Giugiv Casey, "Beyond Total Immersion," *American Journalism Review* (July/August 1999), 3033.

10. Ibid., 33.

11. Koppel, 12.

12. Neil Hickey, "After Monica, What Next?" *Columbia Journalism Review* (November/December 1998), 3038.

13. Richard Lambert, "Rebuilding Trust," *Columbia Journalism Review* (November/December 1998), 39.

14. Judith Valente, "Do You Believe What Newspeople Tell You?" *USA Weekend* (May 1997)*http://www.newseum.org*

15. Grossman, 38.

CHAPTER 15

The Future of News in Eastern Europe: A Study of Promise and Potential

Bailey Barash and Ioana Avadani

The year 2000 marked a decade since Romania freed itself from the devastating rule of Nicolau Ceausescu. At the end of 1989, amid a rain of bullets, student-led Romanian protesters took to the streets to fight for the overthrow of Ceausescu's communist government. A thousand people lost their lives, and the uprisinsg was seen on television around the world. Ceausescu and his wife, Elena, were promptly executed, but the newly elected leader and his party weren't able to establish effective paths to economic reform.

Bailey Barash is an independent television producer who produces features and documentaries on a variety of social issues, including cross-cultural aging and critical decisions at the end of life. A former executive producer for CNN, in 1998 she was the recipient of a Knight Center Press Fellowship at the International Center for Journalists. Ms. Barash traveled throughout four former Eastern Block countries: Romania, Slovakia, the Czech Republic and Hungary. In the process, she interacted with newspaper, radio and television journalists, teaching and learning along the way.

Ioana Avadani is the director of the Center for Independent Journalism in Bucharest, Romania. As a reporter, she covered the refugee situation in Albania and Macedonia for the Voice of America and continues to provide commentary about Romanian politics to the network. She has been a news producer for PRO TV as well as the deputy editor in chief, in charge of the international desk, for the Mediafax wire service.

Ms. Barash and Ms. Avadani met during the spring of 1998 when both were in Romania. What follows is a collaboration, told mostly from the point of view of Ms. Barash's experiences as an American journalist in a part of the world where press freedoms are threatened.

The country languished in poverty and floundered as people tried to figure out how to live and prosper in a free society.

The old communist rule had demanded strict self-censorship not only of journalists, but also of every citizen. Each person was obligated to spy on his or her family, colleagues and neighbors, and report any critical conversation or wrongdoing to the Securitate secret police. It was hoped this would all change with the fall of communism.

According to Romanian media observers, after 1991, many new journalistic outlets blossomed in the country, as writers, editors, reporters and entrepreneurs joined together to establish newspapers and entice investment in the growing number of upstart independent radio and television stations. However, unlike other Eastern European countries such as Hungary, the Czech Republic and even Bulgaria—where all the print media is in German hands—Romanian media has been hindered by a poor show of interest from foreign investors.

Initially, Romanians enjoyed the new luxury of easy access to news and information, and read, on the average, two newspapers a day. The government supported the media, because positive articles had helped them get elected. Politicians took this mutual admiration for granted and ultimately were shocked and outraged when journalists they considered "friends" started to criticize their political and professional performance.

As citizens assessed the magnitude of the devastation and poverty that was Ceausescu's legacy, and editors realized their potential customers were too poor to buy a newspaper every day, the originally solid circulation numbers for the dailies shrank.

The media have come under even more pressure, because the supposed democratic society of Romania continues to foster a rich culture of secrecy.

International media observers say Romanian journalists are hindered by severe restrictions on their ability to report the news as it really happens. There is still a crackdown on those who would criticize the country's decision makers. Journalists claim the guarantees of freedom of speech, as stated in the Constitution, are not supported by the Parliament; in fact, journalists who attempt investigative reporting on alleged government corruption are subject to a pattern of persecution and arrest under Romania's Criminal Code.

The Parliament continues to support laws that make it possible to sue journalists for disseminating information that is considered a threat to national security, a claim of police misconduct or criticism of government officials and actions. The number of lawsuits against journalists is on the increase, and policemen or judges file many of the claims.

Currently there is no way to legally limit what the government or industry chooses to call a "legitimate state secret." Releasing officially restricted information is judged as a criminal offense, and if found guilty, journalists can be jailed and fined. As a consequence, critics say the news content available to Romanians is considerably weakened and distorted, and the average citizen is under a heavy bombardment of pseudo-information, attractively formatted in print, on the Internet and on television, but with little impact.

And yet most news spreads. The common expression used is: "Nobody tells, but everybody knows." This is due in part to the ready availability of mobile phones by which reporters tap their confidential sources like ministers or advisers willing to get immediate but anonymous confirmation of information gathered elsewhere.

Some of my own impressions of Romania, as a visiting journalist in the spring of 1998, bear witness to claims of distortion of the news, and some do not. I went to Romania as a Knight International Press Fellow of the International Center for Journalists. My host was Ioana Avadani, co-author of this article and the Executive Director of the Center for Independent Journalism (CIJ) in Bucharest, Romania.

CIJ was established and is supported by The Independent Journalism Foundation, an international nonprofit organization that encourages the growth and development of the free press and generation of balanced, accurate, unbiased news reporting through media workshops, seminars, lectures and training in countries where media is attempting to free itself from the bonds of censorship and government control.

During my three-week stay, I worked with crews at several TV stations, government and private, and talked with news editors and reporters at some of the major Romanian newspapers. I found that many of the newer media outlets in Romania started their operations with state-of-the art technologies. They have the capability to look and sound like Western TV and radio stations. The most popular newspapers have tabloid layouts, with color pictures of scantily clothed women on the front page. In a population of 23 million, everyone has television, and cable TV is very popular. Independent, commercially broadcast TV is dominated by a network called PROTV, which is supported by heavy Western investment. Other independent commercial networks are ANTENA 1 and PRIMA TV. In all but the larger cities, the stations' budgets can only afford about three hours of original programming a day. Most of the day's programming is films and syndicated entertainment.

News about politics and government makes up most nonentertainment programming, and attracts large audiences.

Program production values are strongly influenced by the technological capability of the equipment and the experience of the directors, with less emphasis on editorial balance and objectivity. The state TV network, TVR, has a large budget, but its own news programming looks flat compared with that of the independent stations.

I met students, reporters, assignment editors, producers, writers, photographers, news directors and station managers and owners in the country's capital, Bucharest, and in several smaller cities and rural locations. At the commercial, independent outlets, the staff works as long and as hard as any employees at a local American station. At the state-owned network in Bucharest and its network stations in other large cities, the pace can be a little more leisurely and the approach more institutional. There, the level of energy and enthusiasm depends on how much creative license and independence the staff are given, and since the TVR is a voice for the government, little is left to independent thinkers.

The media's technical preference is for digital, computerized equipment, if they can afford it. In the small, struggling cable outlets they often get by with consumer-grade, "high 8" cameras and VCRs for editing. Most stations have at least one computer and some e-mail and Internet access. In the larger, better-bankrolled operations, the equipment ranges from a combination of analog and digital to all digital. Even with a very basic operation, the crew and staff push their capabilities to the maximum and produce well-conceived, if not well-executed, products.

Most towns have at least one privately owned radio and TV station. At many stations, the staff is young and smart, but not professionally trained or educated as television news journalists. They are learning on the job, and if they are motivated and have the support of their bosses, they can also benefit from working with outside trainers and consultants in local workshops. These are run by a substantial number of international nongovernmental organizations, which offer technical, financial and professional help, including the Open Society Foundation, Freedom Forum, the BBC, the Independent Journalism Foundation and the International Center for Journalists. They are encouraging the potential that is there for excellent producing, writing and reporting in Romania.

At many small stations the photographers are men in their forties and fifties who learned their skills as film cameramen in the communist era. They were trained in a cinematic style, which results in very aesthetic shots, and they believe, for the most part, that the reporter or producer has no right to interfere with their artistic endeavors. At the larger stations, where the photographers are likely to be as young as the rest of the staff, the style is a combination of Western news shots and MTV-type camera moves, and field production is more of a collaborative effort.

Much of the news is generated in press conferences called by local or national government, industry or law enforcement officials. In this setting, journalists are invited to sit around a long conference table and are served coffee and bottled water until everyone is ready. Video cameras are set up behind the journalists. The official comes in, sits at the head of the table and talks, uninterrupted, for as long

as he or she wants; then he or she may or may not take questions.
The officials do not speak in sound bites. The response to a question
could be as long as the original speech. On the other hand, public
authorities do not see themselves as accountable to those they represent, and a probing question can easily elicit no answer. Critical
reporting of an event can close the door to future interviews and
information for that journalist.

Interviews behind the face of authority are also harder to get
than in Western countries. Many people are suspicious and don't
want to be perceived as being a critic or a snitch. On the other hand,
the media consumer in Romania expects the media to have a strong
opinion about everything. The audience is looking for guidance on
how to feel about a situation, on what stance to take. They often get
what they wish for, because a lot of the news reporting is built on
opinion rather than on an objective, balanced flow of information.
Unbiased reporting requires access to facts, the most valued, and
least available, commodity in the country.

Even if the information is available, continuity can get mangled
in the editing process. I saw many news reports air with one reporter's
voice on a story's recorded narration and another reporter on-camera
in that same story. At times the only visible evidence of a reporter is
a disembodied hand holding a microphone up to the interviewee.

There is a definite contrast between the ethics of Western and
Romanian news gatherers. There are no generally accepted ethical
standards for journalism in Romania. For example, the larger
Romanian television stations take pride in their ability to broadcast
live and use that tool as often as they can in their news shows.
However, once in a while the producers and directors will use a
"fake" live shot if it improves the look of their show. If something is
not really happening at the right moment, shots might be set up to
add to the impact of a story. Sometimes reporters and crews consider
these measures acceptable.

On one of my visits to an independent station in Bucharest,
reporters were doing follow-up stories on a gas leak that caused an
explosion at an apartment house the day before. Four telephone

linemen were killed in the blast. It was a telling example of decay of the infrastructure, in this case the large gas pipes that supply buildings in the city. There was a video of the aftermath of the explosion, including the body of one of the victims, and the piece was accompanied by a studio interview with the head of Romanian Gas.

During that interview they showed another report, a sidebar about another location in the city where people smelled gas leaking from pipes buried just under the dirt. The video showed a man smoking, then throwing the lit cigarette on the ground, followed by a burst of flames. The head of Romanian Gas floundered as he searched for a satisfactory response to the situation. The video was quite spectacular and effective; the embers ignited a real gas leak. I pointed out that the sequence should have been identified as a demonstration or simulation in the report. However, my ethical concerns, from the point of view of a Western journalist, made little or no sense to the Romanian crew.

Newspapers are also prone to sensationalism and opinionated reporting that often supports the political and economic leanings of the owner. Prejudicial, stereotypical terms are accepted in pieces on some minorities, especially the Gypsies, called Roma, in Eastern Europe. They are repeatedly presented in a negative, discriminatory light.

In Iase, a city in Eastern Romania, I met with representatives of a news network that is trying to break the hold of communist-style oppression on the media. The Nord Est Media Group includes newspapers, weekly magazines, TV stations, radio stations, Web sites and marketing and sales operations. Its newspaper, *Monitorul*, is the largest regional newspaper in Romania, with 15 daily editions. A computer network links its news outlets. Editors in each location can post their articles and transmit digital color photographs. All the newspapers are printed in Iasi and distributed by car every morning. With no front-page cheesecake photographs, the newspapers emphasize the local news, color photographs included.

The information inside is repositioned in each town's newspaper according to its importance to that town. The same articles about

national issues can appear at different lengths in the different
regional editions. Each edition is complete in itself, with local clas-
sifieds to support it. Like many of the Romanian publications,
Monitorul has its own Web site, which includes an English language
edition. And like many Romanian news outlets, *Monitorul* has had
its share of arrests and fines and incidents of harassment for negative
reporting about the power brokers in government, the legal system
and industry.

Romania wants desperately to follow other former Eastern
Block countries, like Hungary, into NATO and become a viable part
of the European Union. Officials say, "We wish to conduct an active
foreign policy to dismantle for good the vicious circle of isolation,
on the one hand, and of the fear of what is foreign, on the other
hand." Many of the news and information outlets born in the 1990s
in Romania are attempting to break through that curtain of isolation
and help bring Romania into the 21st century. Their dedicated
efforts tell a story of promise and potential.

CHAPTER 16

Bridging the Digital Divide: Leading the Disenfranchised into the Information Age

Allison Davis

He walked confidently down the city street. As he passed the store windows he looked approvingly at his reflection; his fitted hat from Lids ($20); his solid gold chain with its heavy medallion ($200); his Hawaiian print shirt ($45) over his Old Navy tee ($10); his Johnny Blade oversized jeans ($75); his new Michael Jordan's ($150); and to top it off, his leather Averex jacket ($500). Much of what he had on, he had begged and pleaded for and his mom heard those pleas. Despite her economic struggles, she wanted her child to be "hip," current. And she was willing to work hard to pay the price. "It was money well spent," he thought to himself as he attracted the eyes of his many admirers. He was clean! He was cool. He knew the words of dozens of rap songs; had beaten every video game from Myst to Zelda. He yearned for a cell phone. Yet, he was slipping through the digital divide.

The U.S. government tells us that there is a "digital divide": techno-haves and have-nots. This divide between those with access to new technologies and those without has been described as one of

A former writer and producer on NBC's "Today Show," as well as the "NBC Nightly News," Allison Davis has a long and distinguished career in journalism. She was the executive producer of MSNBC from its inception in 1994 until 1997. Currently, she is Vice President, Creative, of Dunbar Productions and CBS, Inc. Ms. Davis is also a founder of the National Association of Black Journalists.

185

the world's leading economic and civil rights issues. Yet, people of color have certainly embraced technology. Recent studies indicate that the use of cell phones, pagers and cable television by America's minorities nearly matches general usages. It seems safe to say that folk find a way to keep in touch and be entertained.

The number of minorities online continues to increase. According to the third Forrester Research survey, 50 percent of Hispanic households were using the Internet, compared with 45 percent of white households. In 1999, Hispanics were narrowly ahead, but the numbers from a survey done early in 2000 indicated the trend was continuing. Also ahead of whites, Hispanic households accessed the Internet from every category of location—homes, work, schools and libraries.

Among African-Americans, 35 percent of households were online in 2000, up from 23 percent in 1999—an increase of almost 50 percent in one year. In fact, according to *Cyber Dialogue,* nearly half of African-Americans online were under age 30 and the average annual income of those online was $58,300. But what are we doing online? *Cyber Dialogue* says minorities were significantly more likely than the general online population to seek sites on entertainment (music and gaming). That's discouraging given the vast news and information resources that exist online.

In the turbulent 1960s and early 1970s, African-American activists were among those who encouraged young people to question authority. During those days, many of us sat around in small apartments discussing the latest news of the day and the impact it would have on African-Americans. We clipped articles from local newspapers that proved or disproved a political point. We grew skeptical of the news reports we heard, saw or read, "knowing" that they reflected the "white man's view." We yearned for more voices, varied voices. We visited newsstands that had a large variety of periodicals and read quietly in the corner so we wouldn't have to pay outrageous prices to read this often hard-to-get "foreign" news. We wanted perspective and depth. We traveled miles to hear lectures, waited days to get transcripts, stood by weeks to get our hands on obscure books and writings. We thought globally though global news and information was hard to come by. We didn't want the homogenized version of revolution. We wanted to see its whole; dissect it and adapt it. We needed to live in a digital world.

When I first went online more than 15 years ago, I felt an extraordinary power racing through my veins. Compared to today, there was not much available, but what was online seemed to make me smarter, more informed, so very "hip." I was a subscriber of the *Source* (which was later bought by Compuserve/AOL). With my Apple IIe and my 300-band modem, I could access news from around the world. United Press International made early strides in the home digital market.

Access was painfully slow and it hung up my one phone line for hours, but there were interesting communities emerging that offered me the voices I so yearned to hear. "The Well" and "PeaceNet" had links to people and places not served by telephones. There were no pictures, just text. No animated GIFS, just information. No sound or video, but it was ever so sweet to know that the information was uncensored and ready to be interpreted by me.

The United States steps up the pressure on South Africa to end apartheid and I've got the "straight dope" from the African National Congress. The U.S. embargo on Cuba brings additional hardships to that small communist nation and I can interact with those living those hardships. Armed with this information, I was able to fill in the picture painted by a more established American press.

As a journalist, the depth of information gathered in this wonderful digital world enhanced every story I told. A series on education I helped produce with the online help of the Education Resources Information Center won numerous awards. As a result of the depth of the questions found online, an interview with former Attorney General William French Smith netted some surprising responses.

E-mail was relatively new, but through it, I was led to other information resources. My e-mail moniker was nothing cute like alleycat@whatever.com, but it was a series of numbers given to me randomly by the Internet Service Provider. It was not something you put on your business card. It was not something that became part of your identity. It was the way to route messages.

I found gathering information through e-mail was much easier than reaching people by phone. Thinkers and doers had e-mail. They were people with a message or a cause. There was no spam back then; no worries about messages advertising x-rated material or get-rich-quick schemes. There was dialogue, and long, thoughtful responses to burning questions. Online, I found resources, references and answers. It was simple back then. No glitz. And when I was alone, facing the daunting screen filled with information meant solely for my eyes, there was a feeling of power brought on by almost instant enlightenment.

In Africa, the Internet has helped journalists oppose oppressive regimes. Joe Kadhi, a journalism professor at the University of Nairobi and former managing editor of the *Daily Nation,* said that prior to 1990, if any journalist wrote anything against the one political party in Kenya, "it was as good as committing suicide." His paper covered political demonstrations despite a ban by Kenya's president. "We were the only paper with the story," Kadhi said.

A few years later, the Internet came to Nairobi, allowing journalists to write stories they never would have been able to write before. There's been a change in the political climate now that the president knows that his nation's news is easily accessed through the World Wide Web. The president's concern about "the whole world watching" has given the media in Kenya more freedom than ever before.

I've watched as my own children discovered the power of the Internet. One child had to compare and contrast poet Langston Hughes with playwright Lorraine Hansberry. Hansberry, a writer in the 1950s, had penned the award-winning drama "A Raisin in the Sun." Hughes began writing in the late 1920s and was a poet of the Harlem Renaissance. On the Web, he found obvious contrasts. Hughes was a man; Hansberry, a woman. Hughes began writing

early in the century; Hansberry, in the middle of the century. However, both dealt with the lives of African-Americans in a white society and the complex issues that surrounded culture and race.

As my son dug deeper, exploring link after link, he came upon
a full text of the famous play. In the introduction of "A Raisin in the
Sun," Hansberry quotes from one of Hughes' most famous poems,

> "Harlem":
> What happens to a dream deferred?
> Does it dry up
> Like a *raisin in the sun*?
> Or fester like a sore—
> And then run?
> Does it stink like rotten meat?
> Or crust and sugar over—
> like a syrupy sweet?
> Maybe it just sags
> like a heavy load.
> Or does it explode?

As he scrolled through the dialogue, he noticed many phrases
had been hyperlinked. Clicking on the highlighted phrases, he realized that he was taken back to sections of the poem by Hughes that
had influenced a great playwright (Hansberry) and been the genesis
of an extraordinary piece of work. My son saw the link; the thread
that tied these two writers to each other. Chances are days and weeks
at the public library could not have reaped such remarkable results.

As my son later learned, there is danger in too much information. He had a school project requiring him to write about the presidential candidates and their positions on various issues. For hours,
he painstakingly reviewed scores of links offered by Yahoo!. He
poured through online newspapers, magazines, news channels and
candidates' Web sites. Eyes glazed over, he dug deeper, moving on to
the sites of interest groups and fringe groups.

He listened to streaming video and audio, read transcripts and wound through various bulletin boards. He clicked and he highlighted, and when he could take it no more, he simply shut down. I'm not sure how much he retained of what he read, saw or heard, or if he was able to separate the wheat from the chaff, but this is one time access did not translate into power. For him, it translated into confusion.

Truth is, digital technology has put more knowledge and information within reach of more people than any other invention known to man. The information it carries can topple a government or strengthen a family. Universal access will come as companies cut the cost of hardware and software to tap into the buying power of the world's minorities. The main barriers to computer and Internet adoption are both simple and complex. Because they build it, doesn't mean all will come or all will feel welcome when they get there.

There's still a lack of understanding of the benefits the Net can bring or of the vast amount of information distributed by these technologies. And maybe there's unwillingness by too many minorities to explore. To dig deeper. To think globally. To seek answers to the harder questions. To interact. They feel the Internet offers more confusion than enlightenment, more fun than facts, more skepticism than certainty. The problems with traditional media don't go away under this new media model. There's room to be heard, but who's talking?

According to the Freedom Forum, during the 2000 election year, few major sites focused on African-American politics. Well-known sites oriented toward African-Americans offered little news, and much of what they offered came from mainstream white media. Web sites like *NetNoir* and *BET.com* have no news staff and virtually no African-American voices other than users' comments on bulletin boards.

But new voices are emerging. Slowly. *PoliticallyBlack.com* bills itself as the official online source of African-American politics. In addition, it provides the user with a long list of links to political candidates and online election resources. The Black Information Link describes itself as "the premiere UK site for ethnic minority issues." It's actually a voice for minorities living in Great Britain and links to similar sites for African-Americans living in Europe. But it's not easy to find these sites. They don't have the big budgets of a *New York Times* online or even a *BET.com*. Popular search engines may provide a link if you know how to search.

So, the challenge is not to get computers into the hands of minorities. That will continue to happen at a rapid rate. The challenge is to help minorities and the disenfranchised become information consumers—seekers of information—and open to the variety of voices that will hopefully find their way in this emerging digital environment.

INDEX

193

Open Society Foundation, 181
Orbit Communications Group, 32
Orbit Networks, 108
O'Reilly, Tony, 87

Pack journalism, need to avoid, 61
Participatory democracy, application
    to news, 115
Partisan bias, 66
Perot, Ross, 58
Persian Gulf War, coverage of, 18, 46,
    171
Petrovich, Jon, 22
Pickering, Susan, 161
Planet Syndications, 96
Pocket book issues, 3
PoliticallyBlack.com, 190
Pravda, impact of collapse of
    communism on, 142
The Press, 96
Press conferences, generation of news
    in, 181–82
PRIMA TV, 180
"Project Vote Smart," xvii
Protocol news, focus of Egyptian news
    reporting on, 106
PROTV, 180
Public radio, 113–14, 122–23
    BBC contribution to, 114
    differences between BBC and,
        114–15
    driveway potential and, 115
    role of hosts on, 114–15
Public Radio International (PRI), 116

Quayle, Dan, 58

Radio Monte Carlo, 108
The Radio Network, 93–94
Radio news
    fusing contrasting cultures in,
        113–23
    in New Zealand, 93–95
Radio New Zealand, 94–95
Regionalization, 28–31
Reuters, 18, 95, 148–49
    in New Zealand, 90

Robertson, Nic, 16, 24
Romania
    ethical standards for journalism in,
        182
    news coverage of, 177–84
Romanian Revolution (1989), 66–67,
    69–70

Satellite news services, in Egypt, 110
Satellite phones, 62–63
Satellites, in CNN coverage, 18–19
Satellite techniques, 170–71
Schneiderjohn, Diane, 30–31
Serbia, NATO action against, 18
Sex scandals, 60
Showtime, 128
Shuster, Alvin, 10, 141–45
Silvia, Tony, xiii, 3–12, 165–75
Simpson, John, 90
Simpson, O. J., 57–58
"60 Minutes" in New Zealand, 92
SKY Television, 32, 87, 171
Smith, Red, 133
Smith, William French, 187
Society of Professional Journalists, 174
Sound bites, 70–71
Soviet Union
    CNN coverage of, 46–47
    collapse of, 10, 18, 147
Sponsorship, 41
Sports coverage for international
    audience, 58
Sports Illustrated, 21
Sports Illustrated on the Web, 21
Spot-news coverage, 71
La Stampa, 143
StarTV, 32
Stereotypes as problem in news
    coverage, 55–56
Stewart, Robert, 26
Stock market movements, 151
Stringers, 93, 116, 121, 136
    news media reliance on, 137–38
Stylebook CNN, 38
Sueddeutsche Zeitung, 144
Sullivan, Stacy, 9–10, 135–40